THE CENTER WILL HOLD

THE CENTER WILL HOLD

AN ALMANAC OF HOPE, PRAYER, AND WISDOM FOR HARD TIMES

CHRISTOPHER DE VINCK

LOYOLA PRESS.
A JESUIT MINISTRY
Chicago

LOYOLA PRESS.
A JESUIT MINISTRY

3441 N. Ashland Avenue
Chicago, Illinois 60657
(800) 621-1008
www.loyolapress.com

ISBN: 978-0-8294-4930-3
Library of Congress Control Number: 2020933327

Printed in the United States of America.
20 21 22 23 24 25 26 27 28 29 Bang 10 9 8 7 6 5 4 3 2 1

To Roe

Contents

Introduction

In Wallace Stevens's poem *Prelude to Objects*, he wrote about the stairs, that "sweep of an impossible elegance." I think of our lives as a grand sweep of stories, an impossible elegance rolled out before us as we manage each day with hope and courage. How we interpret these ordinary stories defines who we are as people of faith.

British journalist Malcolm Muggeridge wrote, "Every happening, great or small, is a parable whereby God speaks to us, and the art of life is to get the message."

I have been to Paris; I have been to Rome. I have been to London, Brussels, Copenhagen, Vancouver, Portland, New York City. I've traveled to Austin, San Antonio, Chicago, Los Angeles, Seattle, Atlanta, Grand Rapids, Fort Lauderdale, Denver, but no place is more exotic to me than the stories of my past, parables with hidden messages filled with the elegance of my grandfather tending to the rose garden or the stillness of a praying mantis on the grass.

When I was a boy, my grandmother took half a sleeping pill before going to bed for the night. She took only half because she feared that the side effects of a whole dose might ravage her fragile stomach. It was my job to split the pill and pour a glass of water for her as she prepared for bed. Often, after my grandmother swallowed the pill and drank her water, she would sit on the edge of her bed, smile, and show me once again the picture of my grandfather that she had on her nightstand.

He died many years before she did, but each night she said a prayer beside his photograph, and each night she looked at me and smiled with great pride and love for the man she had been married to for over sixty years.

Each night my grandmother told me a small story about her husband: how he rode his horse in the parks in Brussels in his general's uniform, how he survived World War I and World War II, how he loved to plant roses in the garden. Those stories comforted my grandmother before she slept, and then in her sweet, soothing voice she blessed me with a small, invisible sign of the cross that she placed on my forehead with her thumb.

"A cross and a sleep-well" she'd say in Flemish, and then my grandmother lifted her old legs into her bed, pulled her covers to her chin, and smiled. I'd kiss her good night, click off her lamp, and in the subdued darkness I'd see her adjusting her pillow, and I'd see my grandfather looking back at her from the picture frame, and then I'd quietly leave the room and close the door behind me.

This story of my grandmother still sustains me before I go to sleep as I remember her message of love, and as I remember her blessing on my forehead.

Did my grandmother dance a waltz with my grandfather in her dreams each time she fell asleep?

It is in the parables of our lives that we can seek to understand the wisdom that these messages bring. But how do we enter this place of wisdom now that it seems our world is falling into a Godless time? How do we switch our minds from the troubles of the day to the comforts of the soul?

The poet Luci Shaw said that "we have a 'now you see Him, now you don't' God. We have Himself clothed in visions, in dreams, in metaphors, in parables, in the poetry of the Bible, and in all the ordinariness of the lives we live." That is where we find answers: in the ordinariness of the lives we live.

Often, during my talks across the country, someone invariably comes up to me and says, "Oh, Dr. de Vinck. I like your stories so much. They remind me of so many of my own memories. I like how they sound. They soothe me, they remind me of my own past and my own moments of happiness."

Time and time again people tell me that my essays conjure up images of their childhood, or their grandmothers, or their happy summer memories when they were young. People look at my books and then review the albums of their lives and take delight in the nostalgia of goodness. That is where we find comfort for our souls: in the messages that we are given as we live through our life parables. We just have to learn how to see and listen.

At the end of the day we seek peace. I thought about people coming to me and saying how my books remind them of their own memories. I thought about how the memories of my grandfather and his photograph guided my grandmother to sleep.

Perhaps I can guide you to interpret your own stories, those precious memories that will remind you that the past offers hints of what is holy and comforting. A parable is a story filled with wisdom that will guide us along the way. Our memories store those parables and will protect us in the future when we need them. Perhaps I can recreate my grandfather's soothing presence for all who read this book.

As Tennessee Williams wrote in his play *The Glass Menagerie*, "memory is seated predominantly in the heart."

I hope this book helps you to interpret the memorable and somewhat mysterious stories of your own life, that it helps you uncover what is predominantly in your heart: love, acceptance, courage, goodness, and peace. May God bless us everyone.

Christopher de Vinck
Pompton Plains, NJ
January 2018

SPRING

The sun is hot on my neck as I observe
The spikes of the crocus.
The smell of the earth is good.

—Edna St. Vincent Millay

1

Simplicity

For our boast is this, the testimony of our conscience,
that we behaved in the world with simplicity
and godly sincerity, not by earthly wisdom
but by the grace of God, and supremely so toward you.
—2 Corinthians 1:12, ESV

In February 1948, my mother and father arrived in New York from Belgium on the *Queen Elizabeth*. They quickly settled into an apartment in New Jersey, and on his first day of work, my father returned home filled with enthusiasm and said to my mother, "I saw a blue bird! A *blue* bird!"

My mother, finding this to be incredulous, listened with eagerness as my father described the color of the bird's wings and the blue cap of its head. Neither my mother nor my father had ever seen a blue bird before.

A few days later, my mother tells me, she too saw the blue bird, and was as amazed as my father. It turned out, of course, that the *exotic* bird they saw for the first time was the ordinary blue jay. The same thing happened when they saw a red bird. A *red* bird! They had never seen a cardinal before.

If you see an elephant every day, it is just an elephant. If you see an elephant for the first time, it is a giant cartoon with a tail at both ends and ears like pancakes.

Aesop wrote that familiarity breeds contempt. Mark Twain wrote that familiarity breeds children. For most of us, familiarity breeds complacency. We do not look at a tree with awe unless we see the giant redwoods for the first time.

But an oak tree in the backyard that is eight stories high with a trunk as wide as a washing machine is just a tree that sheds acorns and leaves in the fall.

Who looks at an oak tree? But it is a plant right out of a magician's bag! Maple trees, pine trees—can you imagine seeing a tree for the first time? You would believe that we are still living in the age of the dinosaurs.

Do you remember the opening scene in the iconic movie *Jurassic Park*, when the paleontologist sees, for the first time, the brontosaurus? The man is so stunned that he falls to the ground, the very same reaction my son David had when he was a little boy and saw for the first time the gigantic whale hanging from the ceiling in the New York Museum of Natural History.

Sei Shonagon served as lady-in-waiting to the Empress Sadako in Japan a thousand years ago. Little else is known about this woman, except for her pillow book.

A pillow book was a collection of notes that captured the day's events or the thoughts of the writer. Today we call that a diary. What makes Sei Shonagon's pillow book distinctive is her vision, her wisdom, and her humor—and the fact that this collection of notes was written in the eleventh century. What stands out is her appreciation for ordinary, simple things: "Sparrows feeding their young. To pass a place where babies are playing."

Shonagon admired nature and ordinary objects: "Dried hollyhock. Last year's paper fan. A night with a clear moon." She was easily revolted by what she called squalid things: "The back of a piece of embroidery. The inside of a cat's ear." Remember, she wrote these things a thousand years ago. She loved "white, purple, and black clouds, and rain clouds when they are driven by the wind." And she celebrated that "in spring it is the dawn that is most beautiful."

I was startled as I watched each of my children being born. I was startled when I touched a rock from the moon at the Smithsonian Institute in Washington, D.C. I was startled when I helped carry my father's coffin to the open grave in Vermont. The wood of the box brushed against my thigh.

When my cousin came to America for the first time, she called out with glee in the car on our way home from the airport, "Look! A yellow school bus!"

She had seen many movies from the United States, and that is how she learned that all school buses in America are yellow. There are no yellow school buses in Europe, so she was, with the same delight my parents expressed over the birds, charmed to see a *yellow* school bus. No one in America is excited about yellow school buses. They are everywhere and ordinary.

This is why we have artists. They take things that appear to be ordinary and remind us how extraordinary they really are: Robert Frost celebrating birches; William Carlos Williams praising a red wheelbarrow. Painters stop time with their images of the common day: Pieter Bruegel's harvesters, the dancers of Degas, the children of Mary Cassatt.

Do you believe the earth is spinning around the sun! Can you imagine? We are all on a giant ball that is *spinning* in space!

A few years ago, in response to a media request, the people of Chicago recognized that the greatest wonder of the city was their lakefront view and the splendor of Lake Michigan, water they see every day.

Taylor Wang, an American astronaut, wrote about his experience in seeing the earth from space: "A Chinese tale tells of some men sent to harm a young girl who, upon seeing her beauty, become her protectors rather than her violators. That's how I felt seeing the Earth for the first time. I could not help but love and cherish her."

Cherish what is simple. Be in awe of what is great.

I found a blue jay feather on the grass under the bird feeder this morning. I picked up the feather and carefully attached it to a buttonhole on my yellow shirt.

« »
The world is a flower in our hands.
Our food is a grain of wheat.
Our faith is a simple prayer:
"I believe in God the Father."

2

Gratitude

Give thanks to the Lord, for he is good;
—1 Chronicles 16:34

My grandfather, Maj. Gen. Joseph Kestens, was a humble Belgian soldier during World War I. He was shot in the left arm, the force ripping through his nerves and tendons and destroying the use of that arm for the rest of his life. If the German soldier's aim had been truer by a few inches, he would have been killed on that battlefield, and I wouldn't be here today writing these words.

Gratitude is the exclamation point after the narration of our lives. Whether we are grateful for big things (life, liberty, love) or for the small and mundane (the flight of the heron, chocolate, the scent of the sea), we are the only creatures on earth who can articulate a sense of appreciation with words and gestures of thanks.

According to a joint study between the World Health Organization and UNICEF, one in nine people in the world don't have access to safe and clean drinking water. I shower every morning, and I wash my car and sprinkle my lawn with water that I could drink.

According to the UN's Food and Agriculture Organization, one in nine people in the world goes to bed hungry. I often can't decide if I want an orange, a banana, a pear, an apple, or other fruit nestled in the bowl at the center of the kitchen table.

Elie Wiesel, the man who lost his family but not his faith during the Holocaust, wrote: "When a person doesn't have gratitude, something is missing in his or her humanity."

What are the strands of gratitude? How can we trace the first impulse of love, or goodness, or acceptance? The sun is a contributing source of all life on earth. The Hudson River begins at Lake Tear of the Clouds, a small body of water that sits at the base of Mount Marcy, the highest elevation in New York State. Melting snow and rainwater pour down the mountain in the spring and feed the lake, and the lake feeds the streams and rivers that converge and ultimately swirl under the George Washington Bridge, flow past the Statue of Liberty, and rush out into the Atlantic Ocean. Trace our beginnings, and we discover the roots of gratitude.

In Thornton Wilder's 1930 novel *The Woman of Andros*, he wrote: "We can only be said to be alive in those moments when our hearts are conscious of our treasures." America is a cornucopia of richness, a consequence of democracy and laws, and the struggles of reconciling our mistakes with our core national beliefs: liberty and the pursuit of happiness in the recognition that we are created equally under a merciful God.

In Wilder's 1938 play *Our Town*, the character named Emily, having been given one day to return to the world after her death, calls out: "Goodbye Grover's Corners—Mama and Papa. Goodbye to clocks ticking—and my butternut tree!—and Mama's sunflowers—and food and coffee—and new-ironed dresses and hot baths—and sleeping and waking up! Oh, earth, you're too wonderful for anyone to realize you! Do any human beings ever realize life while they live it—every, every minute?"

It's spring. Plant some peas.

《 》

Lord, let me greet this day with gratitude for all that I am,
for all that I know, and for all that I am capable of doing today.

3

Play

Play skillfully, and shout for joy.
—Psalm 33:3

In E.E. Cummings's famous poem "In Just-," he celebrates the balloon seller as the children, Eddy and Bill, "come running from marbles and piracies and it's spring." As the balloon man whistles, Betty and Isbel "come dancing from hop-scotch and jump-rope." I have great faith that children still know how to play in the new spring.

I was a hard-playing baby boomer, lugging the leg of an old kitchen sink around the yard as my brothers and sisters and I fought World War II all over again. The sink leg looked like a machine gun. The curved handle was really the joint fixture that fit under the corner of the sink, but to me it was powerful enough to shoot down imaginary Nazi planes that flew over the backyard in 1961.

The world was, as Cummings said in his poem, "puddle-wonderful." My sister Anne and I made "penny cookies" from mud in the woods with a small cookie cutter. We "baked" them on the roof of the chicken coop, and while we waited for the sun to do its work, we played school on the front steps of the house.

Our neighbors Johnny and Patty would join us as Anne held her hands behind her back and hid a stone in one of them. We three children sat on the bottom concrete step, and when Anne extended her hand before us, she'd say, "Pick one." If we picked the hand with the stone, we advanced to the next grade (or step). The first one to reach college won the game.

We played jump rope and punched out Davy Crockett's fort and colored Donald Duck in the activity books Rosie brought each Friday afternoon while my parents were grocery shopping. Sometimes Rosie orchestrated a hide-the-thimble game. She'd shoo us into the kitchen, hide a thimble in the living room, and then shout "Ready!" It was such fun looking for the thimble on the bookshelf or in the potted plant or on the windowsill. When we couldn't find it, Rosie called out "Warmer" as we drew closer or "Cold, cold," if we were too far from the treasure.

We drew hopscotch boards on the neighbor's driveway with a broken chunk of the chicken coop wall made of gypsum, the perfect chalk.

We played Chutes and Ladders, Candy Land, and Monopoly. Do you remember, in Harper Lee's novel *To Kill a Mockingbird*, how Scout crawled into an old car tire and rolled down the road, and how the children in the book enjoyed play-acting that they were Boo Radley? My sister and I swung on our own tire swing and pretended we were lion tamers in the attic as we coaxed our cat Tiger-Lily to jump from one box to the next. And we bounced up and down on the maple tree branch pretending it was a train on the way to London; the apple tree was an elephant taking us to Bombay.

Fred Rogers wrote, "When children pretend, they're using their imaginations to move beyond the bounds of reality. A stick can be a magic wand. A sock can be a puppet. A small child can be a superhero."

In 1560, the Flemish artist Pieter Bruegel created his famous work *Children's Games*. There, in that 459-year-old painting, we see children playing the exact same way as children of my own childhood: blowing bubbles, walking on stilts, rolling hoops, playing leapfrog, riding hobbyhorses, playing blind man's bluff, swimming, climbing trees, spinning tops, playing marbles and hide-and-seek.

As I write, I hear the neighborhood children chasing one another with water pistols, riding their bikes and scooters while shouting, "You can't get me! You can't get me!"

The windows of my house are open for the first time this spring. I see one little girl with a daffodil in her hand, and she is waving it back and forth, bopping each playmate on the head. "Boing! You're a tiger! Boing! You're a helicopter! Boing, you're an elephant!"

It is spring, and the world is still puddle-wonderful, and every child ought to grow up with tops, marbles, and stilts, and wave a magic daffodil over our heads so that we can all remember what it was like to be a tiger, a helicopter, or an elephant.

« »

*May we remember how to be childlike
in the presence of the Lord.*

4

The Catcher in the Rye

He has saved us and called us to a holy life—not because of anything we have done but because of his own purpose and grace. This grace was given us in Christ Jesus before the beginning of time.
—2 Timothy 1:9

I was a teenager the first time I visited the circus. Most of my friends drove to the shore after their junior prom. I boldly escorted my date to the circus. It is hard to catch a girl's heart by taking her to the circus, but it wasn't a total loss. I loved watching the flying trapeze act.

I remember how a woman in a sequined costume and tights climbed the long, tall ladder, accompanied by a drumroll. A man, also in tights and sequins, followed close behind. Maybe that is how you catch a girl.

The couple stood on a small platform at the very top of the arena, and then the man pushed off, holding the bar, and he became the catcher. The more he pumped his legs, the higher and faster his body moved in a rhythmic, steady pattern back and forth.

At a prearranged moment, the woman leaped off the platform with her bar, and she began to gather momentum in her back-and-forth movements. She was the flier. It was her intention, at one point, to let go of the bar, flip in the air, and be caught by the man.

As in life, there are catchers and there are fliers. The trick is to find out which one we are. I knew from an early age that I was a flier.

When I was a boy, I found on our bookshelf *Scuffy the Tugboat*, the famous Golden Book written by Gertrude Crampton and illustrated by Tibor Gergely. The boy is given a toy tugboat, and he plays with it in a stream, but the boat slips away from him. The little boat is caught in the current of the stream, zooms past cows, and wends its way through the countryside. The boy can't keep up, and the little boat continues on its frightening journey until it comes to the city, where it is about to be pushed out to the ocean and lost forever.

Just as the poor little tugboat is about to be swallowed up by the raging water, a hand reaches out from the last pier in the city. It is the hand of the boy's father, who catches the tugboat just in time. The boat is saved. I was the tugboat.

I was the tugboat. My father died in June 2012, and I still rush down the streams and along the wild rivers making my own way to the deep ocean of my impending death, hoping my father will catch me just in time.

I was just as taken with the story of *Androcles and the Lion*, the ancient Roman story about a slave who escaped and wound up in a cave with a fierce lion. The lion was in agony because it had a large thorn embedded in its paw. Androcles pulled the thorn out and nursed the lion back to health, and the lion became tame and kind.

Because the young man was so lonely for civilization, he returned to Rome, where he was immediately arrested and sent to the Circus Maximus to be devoured by a wild animal. Of course, just before the wild beast was to catch Androcles and kill him, the lion recognized his old friend and caught Androcles in a warm embrace of recognition and gratitude. The emperor was so impressed that he pardoned Androcles and set him free.

I have been a puller of thorns. I have been a flier all my life. I took risks in love. I tossed myself out into the air, hoping someone would catch me. I've been an observer, a husband, father, teacher, and writer flying in and out of the lives of my students in their doubts, flying beside my own children and catching them when they needed a hug or ten dollars.

In his famous book *The Catcher in the Rye*, J. D. Salinger's character Holden Caulfield speaks about standing on a bluff and saving children as they stumble accidentally and nearly fall off the crazy cliff. Holden said that he'd just stand there all his life and be a catcher in the rye. And that's all he wanted to be. I have been on that cliff many times in my life, hoping Holden would be there to catch me as I tried to fly without a safety net.

Teachers, fathers, mothers pull the thorns from the paws of the beasts in the world; they catch the tugboat that is just about to be tossed into the endless sea; they catch the children who are just about to stumble over the cliff with their doubts and sorrows.

I miss my father.

« »

God the Father, catch me when I fall;
Reach out your hand when I am lost;
Save me when I feel like drowning.

5

Laughter

God has brought me laughter,
and everyone who hears about this
will laugh with me.
—Genesis 21:6

My older brother, Oliver, died at the age of thirty-two on March 12, 1980. He was a terrible brother. We never did anything together. He never played catch with me. He never advised me about girls. He didn't help build the tree fort in the woods. He never swapped baseball cards with me or taught me how to fish.

My brother did provide me with some entertaining moments. Because he was blind, I spent many days when I was a boy pretending that I, too, was blind. I'd close my eyes to see how far I could get through the house without knocking down a lamp or table.

Sometimes, at least, Oliver was my Zen guru. He was so quiet. Because he was so intellectually impaired he'd just lie in his bed like a giant doll. I'd sit by his side and complain about my poor grades in algebra, that I liked this girl, Linda, but she ignored me, and if only I had a Plymouth Road Runner, perhaps she'd pay more attention to me.

Oliver never offered advice. So, in his silence I had to discover my own answers to my woes. Algebra wasn't really important, and Jenny, the new girl, didn't care that I drove her to the high school basketball game in my father's Ford station wagon.

See? Oliver was pretty useless when I was a boy. He couldn't even feed himself. It was my job to feed him dinner: pureed fruit, warm soup, or Beech-Nut baby food from a jar. Oliver couldn't chew. He couldn't hold a utensil in his hand. I had to scoop up his dinner one spoonful at a time and touch the spoon to the tip of his lips. My brother would open his mouth. I'd place the spoon and food into his mouth, and then he'd close and swallow. I never split a hero sandwich with my brother. Boys like to do that.

I couldn't even share a drink with Oliver. He couldn't hold a glass. At each meal I had to lift his head from the pillow with my left hand and place the rim of the glass at his lips with my right hand. After Oliver drank milk, water, or juice, I never heard him burp. Brothers like to hear each other burp.

Oliver couldn't even keep himself clean. When my mother and father and my sister and I gave Oliver a bath, you'd think he'd splash his arms up and down in the water for fun. Instead, we just slid him into the tub, and he'd lie there like a large, soggy pillow.

Oliver was born with severe brain damage, a puzzlement that the doctors never figured out. But it was clear that Oliver did not have the ability to learn, talk, or communicate. He couldn't work a slingshot or dress up like Frankenstein's monster and join me for trick-or-treating, or go sleigh riding or light firecrackers back in the woods. We couldn't be best friends. We couldn't do anything together.

What good was he?

For years and years, I watched how gently my father shaved Oliver's stubbled face. For years and years, I listened to my mother say how much she loved Oliver as she combed his hair.

A boy mimics his father and listens to his mother. The great Russian novelist Fyodor Dostoyevsky wrote in *The Brothers Karamazov*, "What is hell? I maintain that it is the suffering of being unable to love."

My father taught me how to love Oliver in the way he slowly pulled down the sharp razor against Oliver's tender skin. Every morning my mother slowly lifted the white shade of the window above Oliver's bed in a manner that was nearly religious as she let in the day's light to spill over my brother's crooked body.

The only thing Oliver could do was laugh. You could walk by his bedroom in the middle of the afternoon, and you'd hear his husky laughter.

The humorist Garrison Keillor wrote, "The highlight of my childhood was making my brother laugh so hard that food came out of his nose."

I would have liked to have been able to play that trick on my brother. But in the end, one of the highlights of my childhood was hearing my brother laugh, and then I'd laugh too.

We did do that well together.

« »

Guide us, Lord, to sing when we are filled with silence,
to laugh when we are filled with sorrow.

6

The Arrival

For unto us a child is born.
—Isaiah 9:6, KJV

In Walt Whitman's famous poem "Song of Myself," he announces his existence to the world and notes how significant a single blade of grass is to the observant eye.

> I CELEBRATE myself, and sing myself,
> And what I assume you shall assume,
> For every atom belonging to me as good belongs to you.
> I loafe and invite my soul,
> I lean and loafe at my ease observing a spear of summer grass.

In the Hebrew Bible we find a description of the Queen of Sheba's arrival: "with a very great retinue, with camels bearing spices and very much gold and precious stones" (1 Kings 10:2, ESV). Sheba came to visit King Solomon with a caravan of valuable gifts, perhaps on a trading mission. "Then she gave the king 120 talents of gold, and a very great quantity of spices, and precious stones. There were no spices such as those that the queen of Sheba gave to King Solomon" (2 Chronicles 9:9, ESV).

In the spring of last year, our son Michael and our daughter-in-law Lauren invited Roe and me for a tour of Greenwich Village to celebrate Roe's birthday. Lauren is a teacher in the public schools in the village; Michael is a fireman in the highly esteemed Jersey City Fire Department.

"Dad, we know how much you like to visit the homes of writers," Michael said. He explained that Greenwich Village is replete with the history of so many writers, and we could, at least, walk past their homes and read historical plaques. And that is what we did.

We saw the home of Edgar Allan Poe at 85 West 3rd Street, where he wrote his famous poem about the raven, "some visitor . . . tapping at [his] chamber door."

Michael consulted his map and took us to 14 West 10th Street, once the home of Mark Twain. The first words of Twain's novel *Huckleberry Finn* are "You don't know about me without you have read a book by the name of *The Adventure of Tom Sawyer*; but that ain't no matter." But it mattered to us because Twain was introducing one of the greatest books in American literature.

For some reason, Michael was nearly bouncing with delight as he took his mother and father from house to house. I said to Lauren that Michael seemed to be in such a good mood, and she said, "He's been looking forward to taking you and Roe on this tour."

"Dad," Michael said, "down this narrow street is where E.E. Cummings lived." The four of us walked down Patchin Place located off 10th Street between Greenwich Avenue and the Avenue of the Americas.

In cummings's famous poem, a little lame balloon man blows a whistle to announce to the children that he is in the neighborhood, and it is spring, and he is selling balloons, and the children come running.

While I was walking ahead with Michael, he turned to me and said, "We have a great birthday cake for Mom."

The tour was over. We took the PATH subway back to Michael and Lauren's apartment in Jersey City. As we sat at the dining room table reminiscing about our day, Michael stepped out of the kitchen with a birthday cake topped with many candles.

"Happy birthday to you," we all sang. "Happy birthday to you. Happy birthday, dear Roe-Mom, happy birthday to you."

Michael placed the cake on the table, and as Roe leaned over to blow out the candles, she paused, looked at the cake and at the blue swirled inscription *Happy Birthday Grandma*. Roe paused again. I looked at the inscription, puzzled, and then Roe exploded with glee.

"What! Grandma? What? Grandma!"

And then it also sunk into my mind. Roe and I were having our first grand-child, and that is how Michael and Lauren announced the news; that is why Michael was chortling all day long during our house tours.

On November 12, 2018, Finnian Chai de Vinck was born: seven pounds, three ounces.

This was far better news than politicians vying for attention. Whitman may have celebrated the arrival of himself, but the de Vinck family celebrated the birth of a boy with lots of hair. I understand the Queen of Sheba brought gems and spices as gifts to the king, but Michael and Lauren brought Finn into the world, a gift to us all, far more precious and valuable than gold and diamonds.

Finnian came tapping, tapping at the chamber door of life. The little lame balloon man whistled far and wide to announce the sale of his balloons, but when Finnian let out his first cry, he announced the beginning of yet another life, another hope for goodness added to this coming new, tumultuous year.

« »

We enter the world with a purity of heart.
May we learn from the children, daily, daily, daily.

7

All Creatures Great and Small

Look at the birds of the air; they neither sow nor reap nor gather into
barns, and yet your heavenly Father feeds them. Are you not of
more value than they?
—Matthew 6:26, ESV

"Do I dare disturb the universe?" T. S. Eliot asked in his famous poem "The Love Song of J. Alfred Prufrock." The advice I'd give the poet is, "No! Don't do it. Leave the universe alone!"

Last spring, I noticed a robin carrying bits of dried grass in its beak as it flew into the rhododendron bush just outside the window of my little office here at home where I write. While I couldn't see the nest, it was clear to me that the robin was well on her way to laying eggs. I found three when I parted the leaves in my investigation a week later. And, soon enough, the eggs hatched.

After a few weeks I thought it would be a nice idea if I took a picture of the young robins that were squawking in the bush. I slowly parted the leaves and found the birds.

Trying to get a good close-up shot, I leaned into the rhododendrons. I was about to click the shutter when the three young birds gave out a loud screech. The mother robin swooped down from a tree like an angry comic book avenger and started circling around me, flapping her wings and screaming at me. The three baby birds, in one explosive flutter, leaped out of the nest and scattered on the lawn. They couldn't fly yet but were filled with anger and fear. The mother bird kept dive-bombing me as the three young robins scurried around the grass and quickly disappeared under the porch. I didn't get that idyllic photograph, and I had just ruined the peace in the little world of our backyard.

That same week I noticed bat droppings on the side of the house and realized that there were bats living under the eaves. I knew bats didn't like water, and I didn't like bat droppings sliding down the clapboard, so I took the hose and sprayed up into the open space under the roof. Eleven bats flew out, and three babies fell to the ground. I felt horrible (and I now realize that bats are protected creatures). I had thought, incorrectly, that it could do no harm just to chase them out of my house and send them on their way.

I picked up the small bats and drove thirty-six miles to the closest animal rescue center, where I was assured that the little creatures would be nurtured and set free once grown. I was also given literature on bats and how not to disturb their existence. I gave the center fifty dollars and a heartfelt thanks for taking away the guilt I felt for ruining the world of that colony of capped crusaders.

A week later I noticed a beautiful spiderweb on the side of the garage. Thinking of E. B. White's famous book *Charlotte's Web*, and having learned my lesson about leaving the natural world to its rightful place in the universe, I left the spiderweb intact.

That night we had a strong spring storm with lots of wind and rain. When I carried out the garbage the next day, I walked around the garage to check on the spider and her web. Gone! A few strands hung on to the side of the garage. Complete destruction. At least it wasn't my fault this time.

In the Bible we are reminded, "Blessed are the meek, for they shall inherit the earth." I can easily think about those young robins and the little bats and the innocent spider that lost its home. I can easily sympathize with the notion that we ought not to disturb the universe.

But wait a minute: There are boring bees chewing into the side of my house, ants are beginning to invade the kitchen, the mosquitoes mimic Dracula the moment I step out onto the deck, the raccoons are scattering my garbage, squirrels are digging up my newly planted flowers, and chipmunks are running in the basement ceiling.

Perhaps the natural world is trying to tell me something. *Get out of town. You don't belong here. You are not one of us. Stop disturbing the universe.*

« »

The earth is my altar; the sea is my holy water;
The air and sun what give me life.
Lord, I celebrate this home each day,
and I give you thanks for what you have created.

8

Husbands

Let your conversation be always full of grace,
seasoned with salt, so that you may know
how to answer everyone.
—Colossians 4:6

Hand in hand, Roe and I were taking our usual Saturday walk when a flock of geese flew overhead in V formation. When she looked up, Roe said, "I wonder why the Canada geese fly that way."

Instead of trying to come up with a smart explanation, I corrected her. "Canadian geese. They're called *Canadian* geese, not *Canada* geese."

Roe insisted that the correct word was *Canada*, not *Canadian*. I insisted the opposite.

In every marriage there needs to be a balance of power: the woman is always right, and the man always believes he is right. The trick is seeing how both partners dance around the illusion.

"All my life," I said, "I've pronounced it *Canadian* geese, and all my life I've always heard it pronounced *Canadian*."

"Your parents," Roe said, "were born in Belgium, and we say that they are Belgian, right?"

"Right. So, I wouldn't say that they are Belgium people. I'd say that they are, as you say, Belgian. See? Canadian geese."

"Well, those geese are not citizens of Canada. They aren't taking a vacation and walking around Chicago or New York with tourist maps under their wings. People aren't saying, 'There go those Canadian geese again.' They are geese, Chris, Canada geese."

"It's all about air flow," I said as I let go of her hand.

"Air flow?"

"Yeah, the geese fly in a V formation because it is easier for the group. The lead bird stirs up the air, breaks it up in a way, and creates a pocket of air for the geese behind to create lift. The air is a bit less dense, and the following geese don't have to work as hard. When the lead goose is tired, it falls back into line and another goose takes the lead position. It's all about teamwork."

Roe looked at me, smiled, and whispered, "Canada."

We continued to walk in silence.

After we strolled up the driveway to the house, I opened the door for Roe, and as we entered, I said, "I'll check the Internet."

"You'll see that I'm right," Roe said, chuckling as I helped her off with her coat.

Canadian, Canadian, Canadian, I said to myself, carrying my flag of certitude to the computer.

There, I discovered that etymologists use the term "Canada geese." Editors at *National Geographic* magazine call them Canada geese. A zoologist said that we just have to accept that we call the geese Canada and the elephants African.

There are Canada tea, Canada balsam, and Canada turpentine. I was tempted to tell Roe that one anonymous person on the Internet said, "In America we call the geese lunch."

I had hoped to enter the living room like the goose-headed Egyptian god of the earth with my triumph. Roe was sitting on the couch reading Thornton Wilder's *The Bridge of San Luis Rey*.

In the end I had to admit defeat. She was right and I was wrong.

"There is a Mexican bird called the Montezuma quail," I said, "not the Montezumian quail. And the Mississippi kite is not called the Mississippian kite. And the California quail is not the Californian quail."

"And?" Roe smiled.

Defeat is always difficult. "And the goose is called the Canada goose."

Roe smiled again and returned to her book.

In China a pair of geese is often given as a wedding gift because geese mate for life.

I sat next to Roe, reached for my newspaper, and thought of the little proverb: "Ego: the fallacy whereby a goose thinks he's a swan."

« »

Blessed are the humble.
Blessed are those who compromise.
Blessed are those who are patient.
Grant me, Lord, humility,
the ability to compromise,
and patience today and each day.

9

Owl

The little owl, the great owl, the white owl...
—Deuteronomy 14:16

Years ago when it was spring and the windows were open and the early crickets were tuning up their rusty fiddles and violins, I heard a distinct flutter out in the small garden. I stepped up to the back door, flicked on the spotlight, and there, sitting on the porch rail like wise judges in their puffy robes, were three young barn owls looking at me perhaps with the same startled gaze that I gave them.

Why is it that we equate owls with wisdom? For most of history, owls were considered ill omens. They warned that Caesar was about to be killed. Owls were a portent of evil in ancient Indian tribes and in European myths and Chinese lore.

Perhaps we didn't like the owl's ability for stealth. Their feathers camouflage their flight, and, because of the shape of their wings, it is almost impossible to hear an owl swooping through the air.

Perhaps to ancient people, the owl, like ghosts and evil spirits, seemed to have the ability to pull the night fears over them like a shroud.

The three owls on my porch quickly ignored me, shook their feathers, preened, scratched the wood rail, and twisted their heads almost in a complete 360-degree motion as if their heads were bottle caps. I suddenly wanted to join the three birds, sit on the rail, and be a future king.

In Disney's version of the great British Arthurian legend, Merlin the wizard turns Wart, the future king, into an owl so that the boy can see the world as it truly is. And Merlin's own pet owl, Archimedes, is a proud, clever, and wise creature. Don't we all struggle to see the world as it is and wish we could be wise creatures?

The Menominee tribe of Wisconsin believed that the owl, disguised as a grandmother, brought them medicines and curing herbs. That's about right. Many grandmothers are owl-like and feathery, and they bring tea and solace when we do not feel well. I like that: grandmother owl.

The smallest owl in nature is the elf owl, weighing just one ounce, and the largest is considered to be the European eagle owl, weighing up to nine pounds.

Each summer, Roe and I spend two weeks in a small cabin in Ontario, Canada. Last year we met a neighbor for the first time, an old woman who had lived for many years in a lovely, rustic house just down the road. Roe and I spoke about our children, and the neighbor shared with us the sad story of how she and her husband retired in that house only two years before he died. "But I still keep going. I like to travel. I've been to Europe, China, all over the world."

Roe then asked the elderly woman, "Of all the places you have visited, what is your favorite?"

Our neighbor looked up at us from her chair and pointed to the floor, "Right here." And then she said, moving her hand to the right, "Out this very window I saw last winter for the first time a snowy owl." Then she smiled.

We seem to have respect for owls: their size, their feathers, and their beauty. Even Rabbit, in A. A. Milne's famous book *The House at Pooh Corner*, recognizes how special owls are. "Christopher Robin respects Owl," Rabbit said, "because you can't help respecting anybody who can spell TUESDAY, even if he doesn't spell it right; but spelling isn't everything. There are days when spelling Tuesday simply doesn't count."

I called Roe to the door to show her the three owls on the porch rail, and just seconds after she, too, admired the visitors, they flew one by one up into the darkness and onto the power line that snaked along the street from pole to pole.

Edward Lear, best known for his lyrical nonsense poetry, made owls famous with his little poem that began "The Owl and the Pussy-cat went to sea in a beautiful pea-green boat. They took some honey, and plenty of money, wrapped up in a five-pound note." And off they went on an adventure, getting engaged, seeking a ring from a chubby pig, and, in the end, "they danced by the light of the moon."

I looked out my window one more time. The three small birds were gone. In the end, an owl is just an owl.

« »

Let me hear the owl in my night's dream.
As I wake for a moment, Lord, and hear your night call:
"I am the way and the truth and the life."

10

Heritage

Through him all things were made;
without him nothing was made that has been made.
—John 1:3

In May of 1940 my mother was eighteen years old. She lived in Brussels, Belgium, with her mother and with Henry her brother. Her father was an officer in the Belgian army, and he was already separated from the family because of the war that had crashed upon the world that spring.

When panzer tanks, Nazi airplanes, and the blitzkrieg overran the small Flanders nation, my mother was so frightened that she begged her mother that they leave before the enemy troops entered Brussels.

So my grandmother, my mother, and my Uncle Henry were suddenly refugees on a train heading south toward France. My mother said that the train had to stop many times because of the invading planes and their bombs.

My mother also remembers the thousands and thousands of people walking, pushing carts, carrying sacks over their shoulders as they overwhelmed the roads, all trying to escape the invading army.

Finally, my mother and her little family arrived in a French coastal town they knew so well: Dunkirk. To my mother, Dunkirk was a place filled with summer memories on the beach. In the history books Dunkirk will long be remembered as the place where more than 300,000 British and French troops were surrounded by Hitler's army and doomed to certain capture and death had it not been for Winston Churchill, who ordered any boat or ship available in England to cross the English Channel and save the soldiers. More than 900 ships carried out this mission that, to this day, is called the miracle of Dunkirk.

So, there was my mother and her younger brother and my grandmother standing in the chaos of Dunkirk in the spring of 1940. The Nazi troops were advancing. More than 300,000 soldiers were pushed into the little town and the surrounding fields, and my grandmother knew that they had to leave Dunkirk as quickly as possible.

Because my grandmother was so familiar with the city, she and her children walked to the bus stop. Funny how we assume things will still work properly during times of a disaster. But sure enough, a single bus was making its way through the swarm of people trying to evacuate the dying city.

When the bus slowly approached the depot, my mother, grandmother, and uncle were at the front of the massive, desperate crowd. Suddenly hundreds of people surged and began to push forward, all hoping to get a seat on the bus. The bus kept rolling forward, slowly, slowly, when, because of the huge push from behind, my mother was thrown under the bus between the front and rear wheels.

With the bus still in motion, with the chaos and shouting, with the mob pushing forward, my grandmother screamed out to the driver "Stop the bus! Stop the bus!"

The bus driver heard my grandmother, and when he stepped out onto the street he started screaming back at her, angry that she was arrogantly demanding that he stop the bus. But then my grandmother quickly pointed and sobbed in a plaintive cry: "My daughter. She is under the wheels!"

The bus driver stooped down, and there was my mother, on her back with the rear wheels already on her outstretched dress. The bus driver had to use a pair of scissors to cut my mother out from under the large, heavy wheels. Because the crowd was so packed, he could not drive the bus in reverse.

Because of this terrible shock to my mother and grandmother, the driver gave my family the first seats on the bus. Seconds later my mother would have been crushed to death. Seconds later I would not have been born. Seconds later my children would not have been born.

We are precariously linked to people we never knew. How fragile our own existence is, so dependent on the lives of our ancestors, making their own way and surviving.

Remember Clarence the angel in the film *It's a Wonderful Life* speaking to George Bailey? "Strange, isn't it? Each man's life touches so many other lives. When he isn't around, he leaves an awful hole, doesn't he?"

In World War II alone, it is estimated that 60 to 80 million people died. Think of all the broken families, the broken lines into the future; think in gratitude for the miracle of our existence.

« »

For the life you have given us, we thank you, Lord.
For the influence we have, we praise you.

11

In Search of the Soul

This is what the Lord says:
"Stand at the crossroads and look;
ask for the ancient paths,
ask where the good way is, and walk in it,
and you will find rest for your souls.
But you said, 'We will not walk in it.'"
—Jeremiah 6:16

Where is the soul of America? It is nearly summer, and once again I take out the American flag in preparation for Memorial Day. The flag is fading: the blues are not so blue, the reds are not so red.

A few weeks ago, I drove from New York City to Knoxville, Tennessee. I had a bit of free time. I was restless. The nation seemed fragile. I brought with me my old GPS, not wanting to get lost on Highway 81 South.

Where is the soul of America? Maybe I can find it, I thought.

Throughout my journey, the radio was filled with fake promises from a political campaign about unifying the country. The only way I think we can unify the country is to rediscover who we are as a nation.

My first stop was the Round Hill Cemetery in Marion, Virginia. I always admired the writer Sherwood Anderson, and whenever I am invited to give a talk I see if there is a writer's home or grave I can visit. I have been to O. Henry's home in Austin, Texas, and Emily Dickinson's home in Amherst, Massachusetts. I visited the grave of Robert Frost in Vermont and the grave of Edna St. Vincent Millay in New York.

Round Hill Cemetery is just that: a tall, round hill. The graveyard's road weaves around like a black ribbon to the very top where there is a simple tombstone: Anderson. Just a few feet from his grave, there is a small cylindrical monument with these words: "Life not death is the great adventure."

Living in America is a great adventure. As Anderson wrote in his most famous book, *Winesburg, Ohio*, "Dare to be strong and courageous. That is the road. Venture anything. Be brave enough to dare to be loved."

I switched channel after channel on the radio while driving through Pennsylvania, Maryland, and Virginia. I picked up radio stations from Kentucky, Alabama, and North Carolina, and all I heard was the voice of a demagogue speaking about fake love and fake unity expressed with words of anger, ego, and self-righteousness.

The people of our nation have diverse backgrounds. We are a nation of immigrants. My parents endured four years of Nazi occupation before coming to America in 1948. America is not about building walls. We ought to be insulted by the disingenuous call for unity because it is actually a call for segregation of the soul from the universal substance that truly unites us all.

When was the last time men from their golden towers read John Steinbeck's *The Grapes of Wrath*? In the novel, the Rev. Casy says to Tom Joad, "Maybe all men got one big soul ever'body's a part of."

I left Round Hill Cemetery and kept driving northwest to Knoxville. At the hotel I asked the desk clerk for a suggested night's entertainment, and she said, "Over at the town of Walland, for sure. It's Friday night. You gotta go hear the Rocky Branch Bluegrass."

I was never a fan of country music. You know, we people from the East Coast: we either like Beethoven or Bruce Springsteen. We eastern snobs find the twang of the steel guitar irritating. But I took up the woman's suggestion, feeling that I was doing my civic duty by taking in the local color as a sophisticated tourist.

According to the most recent census, there are 259 people living in Walland. When I drove to the civic center, I saw an old man and an old woman, walking arm in arm under the parking lot lights to the front of the building. The elderly couple stood ahead of me in the pay-at-the-door donation line. She wore a faded rose-colored dress, and he wore beat-up jeans, worn boots, and a plaid shirt with the middle button missing. They never let go of each other's arm.

I looked at this quiet couple from Walland, Tennessee, and I thought of Ralph Waldo Emerson's essay "The Over-Soul": "Within man is the soul of the whole; the wise silence."

I entered a small room behind the old couple, and I sat down with the droopy-looking audience while two men with fiddles, one man with a banjo, a woman with a bass fiddle, and yes, a man with a lap steel guitar all tuned up their instruments.

I looked at the ten or fifteen people sitting quietly in their metal folding chairs while I sat smugly with my New York shoes and my Ivy League degree tucked deep inside my ego. The musicians wore checkered shirts and ragged jeans. One of the fiddle players hadn't shaved since the Civil War perhaps. I leaned back in my chair as a tolerant observer.

And then the music. Within the first thirty seconds—and I mean within the first thirty seconds—I was startled. Those five musicians must have dropped down from the southern half of heaven, because how they played, the power of the sounds they created, and the passion and beauty they exhibited astounded me. I turned to look at the somber audience. They were all smiling, all radiating a buried youth; the woman in the faded rose-colored dress was tapping her husband's thigh at the beat of the bluegrass music that streamed out into the Tennessee night, and I was humbled and embarrassed that I had thought I was superior to everyone around me.

I've been to Carnegie Hall. I've been to symphonies, the opera, and to some of the most famous Broadway musicals, but none of that stirred me as much as the music of Walland, Tennessee.

The writer James Agee was born in Knoxville, and in his Pulitzer Prize–winning autobiographical novel *A Death in the Family*, he wrote, "We are talking now of summer evenings in Knoxville, Tennessee, in the time that I lived there so successfully disguised to myself as a child."

Maybe we are all one big soul. Life is the adventure. Yes, dare to be strong and courageous. Be brave enough. Dare to be loved. This is the road to unity, not what is being spewed out from the lips of a political charlatan.

We ought not allow empty politicians to diminish our nation's purity of heart.

If a candidate wants to unite the people of the United States, I think he or she needs to rediscover the soul of our country—and the soul of America is in Walland, Tennessee, and she is wearing a faded rose-colored dress, and she'll be listening to the Rocky Branch Bluegrass music this Friday night over at the civic center.

« »

Heavenly Father, remind me that my soul is my true self: honest with my body, and your whisper in my mind.

12

Teach

I will instruct you and teach you in the way you should go;
I will counsel you with my loving eye on you.
—Psalm 32:8

After forty years as a teacher and administrator in public education, I am retiring. A friend recently asked, "What images stand out the most from your many years in school?" Chalk on my sleeve, stacks of student essays to be graded sitting on my desk like rotting meat, a Snoopy Post-it on my briefcase from my student Carly and her signature smiley face a few months before she died of cancer. We gather souvenirs in our minds, memories that stay with us after the journey's end.

Each year, on the last day of school, I'd run to the front of the building to watch the school buses pull out of the driveway as the children waved from the windows on their way to summer and to their futures. Each time, I'd wave from my window, knowing that they didn't see me, but I waved just the same, almost a blessing, wishing them well.

I remember an assignment I gave my English students: "Prepare a class presentation as if you are one of the writers we studied." A girl, I do not remember her name, arrived in class a few days later dressed in an ankle-length white cotton dress. She plugged in an imitation kerosene lamp, sat in her chair, and spoke about her life. "I am Emily Dickinson, and I wrote poems in Amherst, Massachusetts." During her presentation my student recited from memory one of the poems that "she" had written:

> "Hope" is the thing with feathers—
> That perches in the soul—

And sings the tune without the words—
And never stops—at all—

Another image that stands out in my memory is seeing Gloria at her desk.
I spent twenty years of my career in one high school, and as was my habit,
I arrived early each morning and, after I closed the door to my car and
walked along the sidewalk, I'd look inside a first-floor window, and there was
Gloria already at her desk, grading papers, preparing lessons, writing on the
board. Year after year, there was Gloria, a beacon in the education community,
true evidence of a continuity of spirit and professionalism. There was Gloria
expecting the children. I never waved or tapped on her window. You don't disturb a master during her time of preparation.

Teachers live for the moment when a light is illuminated inside the minds and
hearts of their students, like Helen Keller suddenly realizing that the funny symbols wiggling in her hand her teacher was spelling meant "w-a-t-e-r."

My student Jan was an impossible child: loud, recalcitrant, her hair often
disheveled, her detentions after school her second home—and yet she was the
most inspiring reader of *Antigone* I have ever encountered. "My nature is for
mutual love, not hate," Jan called out from the pages of Sophocles. "Friends,
countrymen, my last farewell I make; my journey's done. One last fond, lingering, longing look I take at the bright sun."

And every Halloween I asked my students to sit on the floor in a circle,
and then I would place a lit candle in the center. As the students settled down
and the weak candlelight softly reflected against their eager young faces, I
read aloud:

Once upon a midnight dreary, while I pondered, weak and weary,
Over many a quaint and curious volume of forgotten lore—
    While I nodded, nearly napping, suddenly there came a tapping,
As of some one gently rapping, rapping at my chamber door.
"'Tis some visitor," I muttered, "tapping at my chamber door—
        Only this and nothing more."

Edgar Allan Poe's raven spread its dark wings over the students once more.

Images follow us long after an event is complete: a teacher plucking the feathers of the raven from his hair, a teacher guiding a young Antigone to follow her passion, a teacher privately tipping his hat to his colleague sitting at her desk at 6:45 each morning. A teacher sitting in a chair listening to a young child who slowly absorbs the wisdom of Emily Dickinson. These are the images that linger from the yearbook of my career.

School buses grind off into the future, candles are snuffed. I, too, believe our nature as human beings is to love, not hate; hope does reside in the soul, and so to the teachers and students, my last farewell, and I, too, take one last fond lingering look, and now my journey's done.

« »

Merciful Lord, my guide, my teacher,
I take lessons from the sun you created
and from the day that waits for me.
May I learn again the power of your instruction.

SUMMER

And so with the sunshine and the great bursts of leaves growing on the trees, just as things grow in fast movies, I had that familiar conviction that life was beginning over again with the summer.

—F. Scott Fitzgerald

13

Summary

Now learn this lesson from the fig tree:
As soon as its twigs get tender and its leaves come out,
you know that summer is near.
—Matthew 24:32

Summers belonged to children, or to the children I once knew. I was born into a world with no Internet, no texting, no tweeting, no Facebook or smartphones, video games, or cable television.

Do children these days have midsummer night dreams? Do they swim in creeks, play stickball, fly paper airplanes and kites with long tails? Many of the summers when I was a boy challenged my sisters and brothers and me to come up with things to do.

Have you ever seen a praying mantis? As a child I liked saving the bees that were caught in the half-enclosed porch. I'd place a glass over a frantic wasp thumping against the impenetrable window, slip a paper under the glass, and carry the brown, angry insect to freedom.

I liked listening to the crickets and tree frogs during their nocturnal symphonies. But finding a praying mantis was like finding a rare baseball card in a pack of gum. (Do children care about baseball cards anymore?)

I was out in the front lot, hiding on my stomach under a pine tree during one of our many games of hide-and-seek, when I looked down and saw a miniature dragon crawling past my nose. Its claws were long and crablike. Its head looked like an alien creature. The wings looked like the thin train of a bridal gown.

"Let's keep it," my brother suggested.

"In a box," my sister added.

We agreed in the end to let it go, and then we ran to my mother. "We found a praying mantis!"

Do children these days express awe?

If you never used a rhododendron leaf as a dollar bill to "pay" for "gasoline," you have never been a true child. My brother ran the "gasoline station," which was really the mailbox. We stuffed an old garden hose into the mailbox, and when we rode up on our bikes, my brother would pull the hose out and fill our "gas tanks," and then we'd pay him in rhododendron dollars, those wonderful long, green leaves that were worth a lot to children who believed that we were rich summer tourists.

What is summer without a good book? Today, if I said something about counterfeit money, mysterious notes, arrows, and exploding buildings, kids would probably say, "Cool! Is that in the new video game?"

And I would say, "No, that's in a Hardy Boys mystery, *The Secret of the Old Mill*. It's all about a secret room and a mill rigged with an electric eye, and hidden tunnels. You'd love it!"

Don't children realize that summer is all about sneaking to buy Superman and Batman comic books, forbidden to us because our parents thought Clark Kent and the Batmobile would poison our minds? One summer I bought a Superman T-shirt and rigged an old projector and painted a black bat onto a slide and projected the bat signal onto the trees at night, hoping Bruce Wayne might see that I was in distress.

When I told some kids in my neighborhood about the water rocket I had when I was a boy, they shrugged and drove off on their electric scooters. I wanted to tell the boys about that red-and-blue plastic rocket. I would fill it up with water and wiggle it onto a little nub that locked, and then pump air into the rocket and pull back the release; the rocket zoomed up over the garage, spurting water in a wonderful gushing sound.

"Guys," I wanted to call back as the children disappeared behind the electric garage door that closed with a muted thud. "Guys! The rocket, it was red and blue, and the water gushed out . . ."

Don't kids know that summer is for playing endless games of Monopoly, mixing Kool-Aid on the kitchen counter, building tree forts, baking potatoes in the fire pit we built in the center of the woods?

I loved the freshness of childhood that mingled with the bright summer air.

Mark Twain had it right: "There comes a time in every rightly constructed boy's life when he has a raging desire to go somewhere and dig for hidden treasure."

I think that time for me was the summers of long ago, when the fireflies blinked and Batman disappeared into the safe and hidden night.

« »

Father in Heaven, thank you for my happy memories of summers,
for they protect me during the cold winter months of my life.

14

Retirement

Gray hair is a crown of glory; it is gained in a righteous life.
—Proverbs 16:31, ESV

I had worked with Ira during our careers in education, and when he retired, we promised each other that we would stay in touch. You know how that goes: a pat on the back with warm words of good luck and health. "Let's keep in touch," but most of us do not. We let relationships go when a circumstance, such as retirement, seems to be an insurmountable bridge to maintain a friendship.

When Ira wrote me a letter inviting me to sail with him on the Hudson, I was delighted. Two weeks later, I dressed in my Yankee baseball cap, my new white sneakers, my shorts, and my Columbia University sweatshirt. I carried a cooler of iced tea to the car, and I was off and ready to gad about in a boat, like Ratty in *The Wind in the Willows.*

When we met at the dock, Ira and I hugged, patted each other on the back, and climbed aboard his nineteen-foot sailboat.

"You look well, Ira."

"I feel well."

The boat bobbed back and forth a bit as we took turns stepping onto the bow. "Hold on to anything that is bolted to the boat," Ira warned with a smile.

As we settled into our seats, Ira pulled the cord to start the engine that pushed us out to the edge of the river. When he turned off the engine, we unfurled the sails, adjusted the ropes, and were on our way, pushed by the wind and our need to catch up on each other's lives.

Ira told me about his daughter's continued struggles and joys of living in Israel with her husband and three children. I said that my son was leaving for a new job in California. We both took solace in knowing that our children were pursuing their own happiness and destinies, and we were equally moved that they lived so far away.

Ira told me how much he enjoys sitting peacefully in the synagogue, in part to avoid the telephone, but also to relish the silence, and I spoke to him about the awe I felt when I stood before the tomb of George Washington at his estate in Mount Vernon.

The sails filled with the wind and pushed us slowly eastward across the river.

We exchanged retirement information: the financial ramifications, the benefits of early and delayed retirement. I then told Ira that I'll be sixty-four this Sunday.

"Happy Birthday," he said, then warned, "Watch your head. I'm coming about." The sails slackened, the boat turned just enough for the sails' edges to grab the wind on the other side, allowing us to sail west, back toward the dock.

Ira and I spent the afternoon eating our sandwiches and drinking our tea, and at times we just sat on the boat and looked down at the Tappan Zee Bridge or up toward the Hudson River and into New York State.

"I visited Mystic Seaport, in Connecticut," Ira said out of the silence. "I happened to be there when there was a replica of one of the ships Columbus used to cross the Atlantic. I wasn't expecting an ocean liner, but I was also not expecting to see how small those ships were. They sailed all those days on the ocean, crossing over with little knowledge of what was ahead. I could not believe how small that ship was."

I thought about Ira and me, two men in our sixties, both retired, and how we made our own journeys in our own small boats across the ocean of our lives—marrying well, raising our children, being faithful to our professions as educators.

Emily, in Thornton Wilder's play *Our Town*, plaintively says, "Does anyone ever realize life while they live it . . . every, every minute?"

After we returned and stood on the dock, my friend and I embraced again, and Ira said, "Let's stay in touch."

For three brief hours Ira and I, two senior citizens, realized life as we were living it on the river that flows out into the Atlantic Ocean and disappears.

« »

Lord, help me accept my changing face,
the evidence of old age, and the feelings of loss.
Guide me to your old age home: the promise of salvation.

15

Memorial

Honor your father . . .
—Deuteronomy 5:16

In the 1950s when I was a boy, my father built a sailboat from scratch in the basement. There were many nights when I heard a saw cutting into wood or the rough sound of sandpaper or the rhythm of a hammer.

One of the iconic memories in my family was my father out in the middle of the Canadian lake we visited each year. There he was: a man sitting on the deck, pulling the ropes, adjusting the jib and the mainsail that were engorged with the invisible wind.

I didn't really know my father; he came from a generation of reserved silence in which men went to work and boys built tree forts deep in the woods. My father never asked me about my girlfriends in high school. We never tossed a baseball back and forth.

I remember the aroma of wood that wound up the stairs and into the living room as I watched *The Lone Ranger* on television. I remember the day my father pushed the sailboat out the basement door and into the sunlight for the first time. The azaleas hadn't bloomed yet. The daffodils were just emerging from the loose soil. "This year we sail in Canada," my father announced at the dinner table that night. I couldn't wait.

I looked out my bedroom window in the middle of the night and could see the sailboat sitting on the trailer in the driveway.

I remember sitting in the Ford station wagon with my brothers and sisters that summer as my mother read in the front seat and my father, shaded in sunglasses, chewed gum and drove us and the sailboat to Canada. I liked looking back and seeing the boat following us like a faithful companion.

The mast was red and strong; the sails were whiter than the Canadian clouds. The deck was smooth wood. The fittings were polished brass, the bow a sleek white like the underbelly of a swan. We all took turns sailing with my father: my sisters, brothers, and me.

When it was my turn, I'd sit in the middle seat like a prince, turning now and again to see my father sitting in the back at the till steering the boat, adjusting the sails.

I didn't know my father's inner life. When it comes to revealing our souls to others, we baby boomers quickly advanced beyond the stoic silence of our parents. I didn't know if my father was ever depressed or lonely or filled with defeat. I watched him plant raspberry bushes in the garden. He played tennis, built a weaving loom, and worked in an office somewhere in a large building. And all seemed well each night when I heard his car crunching the small stones in the driveway as my mother announced, "Your father's home."

My father died at age one hundred. He endured a dreadful stroke, lingered for three years, and died in the presence of my mother and brother. My son Michael and I were two of the six people who carried my father's coffin to the grave.

I remember that, once, on one of our summer vacations, Michael, my brother-in-law Peter, and Peter's son Chris were thinking of taking out the sailboat again. It had been ten years since my father had been to Canada, and the sailboat sat unused in the shed. When they yanked the tarp, they quickly discovered that the boat had been chewed by mice and had filled with mold and rot. The sails were shredded, the mast cracked. The sailboat had not survived the Canadian winters in the shed. It was clear that it was finished and not worth repairing at any cost.

"Let's send it into the lake and set it on fire, like the Vikings did," Michael suggested.

"Let's take it to the beaver pond," Peter countered.

"That's a great idea," both Chris and Michael agreed.

They spent the afternoon hauling the boat up a two-mile dirt road to a bit of property my family owns in Canada. There is an active, six-foot-deep beaver pond with a well-constructed dam made of mud and sticks. It was here that my father visited each morning during our two-week vacations when we were children. Here he took delight in watching the beavers. And here, I learned many years later, my father enjoyed skinny-dipping under the bright morning sun.

Peter, Chris, and Michael launched the boat and let it glide to a stop at the left edge of the beaver pond. We all agreed that this was a fitting resting place for my father's sailboat. I didn't think it would sink so quickly.

The following year, I walked to the beaver pond alone. I walked along the ridge of the dam, peered to my right, and there, through the clear water, I could see the sailboat sitting at the bottom of the pond. It appeared to me to be the end of my father's generation. The end of my life as a boy.

Maybe I know more about my father than I realized: he built sailboats, swam with the beavers, drove his children to Canada each summer, and came home every night.

I liked the sound of those crunching stones in the driveway.

« »

Blessed are they who loved us.

16

Keys

I will give you the keys of the kingdom of heaven;
whatever you bind on earth will be bound in heaven,
and whatever you loose on earth will be loosed in heaven.
—Matthew 16:19

When I was a boy, my father gave me a wooden bank: a tall soldier with a tall black hat, a red coat, and a painted smile. What I liked best: At the base was a small, flat door, and in the middle of the door was a hole for a small, flat silver key. "Like this, Christopher," my father said as he inserted the key into the hole to demonstrate how the little lock worked.

I didn't know about secret places until this toy soldier marched into my imagination. This was where I kept the dollars my father slipped to me now and again. And there I kept a map I had drawn that showed where I had hidden a metal box I buried in the yard, and inside that box my first silver dollar, a birthday gift.

In those years, I thought that a key was something used to protect precious things close to my heart, and then in middle school someone stole my lunch money and I was told that I would have to buy a lock and key for my locker.

Keys represent evil. We lock our cars so they will not be stolen. We lock our houses so a thief cannot walk off with our jewels and televisions. We pull metal grates down over our shops each night so that even a herd of crooks cannot penetrate the barriers.

We build walls; we close borders. No entry. Stop. Access forbidden.

My daughter recently had an operation to remove a tumor. On the day of her procedure, I wanted to stop at the church before going to work just to say a small prayer. We always hear about the dangers of the hospital: the infections, the mistakes made.

The morning mist hung in the parking lot like a shroud. I felt gloomy, tired, and anxious for my daughter. When I walked up to the church door, I began to feel, right away, a sense of relief. But when I grabbed the handle and pulled, the door did not budge; it was locked. The church was closed. Wasn't there a time when the doors of the church were always open no matter the time of day? I went back to the car and said a small prayer for Karen there. (She endured the successful operation with courage and pluck.)

I have to unlock the front door to exit my house, unlock the garage door, start the car with a key, pay a toll before a gate allows me to enter the highway, and open my office with a key. The church doors are locked; even heaven is locked.

On my way home one day last summer, I saw to my right on the small country road a sign on a gray sawhorse: *Open.* This is the only fruit and vegetable stand that I have ever seen that is open without a salesperson, without the owner. There's just a small slot in the back door with a sign: *Pay here.*

I leaned over the fresh Jersey peaches and inhaled the aroma of early autumn. The sweet corn was plump and alluring. Tomatoes, cucumbers, plums . . . all jewels waiting to be admired, selected, and placed in the free paper bags that sat on a wood table. I bought four ears of corn, two tomatoes, a cucumber, and four peaches and slid the money inside the slot. Then I carried home my little victory over evil and keys and the thief. *Open,* the sign read, with trust and old-world values of honesty and integrity.

We lock stores, bikes, suitcases, banks, and sheds. We lock our hearts away from each other out of fear we will be robbed, attacked, or hurt.

I still have my small wooden soldier standing as a sentry on my shelf. The lock is broken, the key lost many years ago. I don't remember where I buried my silver dollar, but I do know our lives would be much happier if we lived in a world without keys, a world in which the gates of heaven and the church doors and our homes were never locked but open wide like a vegetable stand with fresh peaches.

« »

I thank you, Lord, for the key to your heart.
I thank you, Lord, for not keeping your love of me a secret.

17

Identity

You were taught, with regard to your former way of life, to put off your
old self, which is being corrupted by its deceitful desires; to be made new
in the attitude of your minds; and to put on the new self, created to be
like God in true righteousness and holiness.
—Ephesians 4:22–24

One afternoon during the summer of 1966, I secretly zoomed downtown on my bicycle. I had money in my pocket and a forbidden mission: I was going to buy a Batman comic book. I remember the thrill of the air pushing against my face as I pedaled down Franklin Turnpike in my New Jersey hometown. I remember how my shirt flapped on my back, adding to the fantasy that I was Batman in my cape on my way to rescue the world from the Joker or the Riddler. I was a boy obsessed with secret identities.

One of the first adult books I read was Emmuska Orczy's novel *The Scarlet Pimpernel*, that wonderful story about the chivalrous Frenchman Sir Percy Blakeney who, with his secret collection of friends, saved people from the guillotine using disguises and skilled swordsmanship. No one knew his identity; he was recognized only by his symbol, the scarlet pimpernel, a common European flower. I pretended that I was the Scarlet Pimpernel wearing a disguise of a paper mustache and a tricorn hat while rescuing my cat from the French Reign of Terror as it slept on the sofa.

When I began to step away from my parents' dreams about their child, I started to develop my own sense of self. I rescued a rabbit from the jaws of the cat. I raised and protected a baby possum that my father found one morning at the bottom of the garbage can. I cupped frantic, desperate moths trapped in the house and gently released them into the night air. I liked helping my grandmother up the stairs, feeding my disabled, blind brother applesauce with a spoon, making breakfast for my mother when she was so ill. I liked that feeling, helping those in trouble: animals, grandmothers, myself.

Much of the thrill was carrying out brave deeds in secret. I liked to sit on the back-porch steps alone, feeding that young rabbit warm milk with an eyedropper.

I liked kissing my grandmother's forehead good night as she slowly closed her eyes. It gave me a sense that she would sleep well through the night, and when I shut off the lights in the room, I lingered for a moment, filled with gratitude that I was alive because of this old, old woman who had endured World War I and World War II, and who loved me for me.

I loved watching George Reeves, the famous television Clark Kent, tugging at his tie as he stepped toward a phone booth, letting the audience know that he was about to change into his Superman costume. I loved hearing the late Adam West, the famous television Bruce Wayne, announce to his sidekick "To the Batcave, Robin." I wanted to be Batman. I wanted to live a double life: one as a happy kid who bought Good Humor ice cream with his sister down at the summer swimming pool, and the other this brooding superhero who invented the Bat-Signal.

In the attic I found an old slide projector. With scissors, cardboard, and tape I made a slide that, when inserted into the machine, projected on the wall the exact outline of the famous Batman spotlight I saw in the comic books. When I aimed the image out my bedroom window, the Bat-Signal was clearly visible against the night sky. Now I had a way to summon Batman when I needed to be rescued. I had a way to project to the world that I was there, available to rescue them from any danger.

I bought my Batman comic book, forbidden contraband in my house when I was a boy because my parents thought comic books would corrupt me and my education. They wanted me to read, well, *The Scarlet Pimpernel.* I rode my bike to the neighbor's farm where there was a small pond hidden under brambles and low trees. There in my own Batcave I followed the brave adventures of the Masked Crusader.

I grew up to become a teacher, wanting to help students unmask their hidden identities as they bravely battled the world's challenges.

We live with myths of ourselves, balancing out the meaning of the Bat-Signal we stoically project to the world each day: rescue me or let me rescue you. Funny how that sounds so much like the definition of what it means to love one another.

《 》

Merciful God, in the mirror I see who I am,
and the person you created.
Thank you for giving me a name; thank you
for the joy of myself. For these things
I praise you and thank you.

18

Wisdom of the Father

Jesus replied, "Anyone who loves me will obey my teaching. My Father will love them, and we will come to them and make our home with them."
—John 14:23

Two months before my father died, I asked him if he had any advice for young people. I thought about asking him after my forty-year career as a high school administrator ended.

I think of the thousands of teenagers I have met along the way, all the good teachers I've worked with, all the parents I have spoken to, and then I recall what my father said in his old age, sitting in his chair, unable to walk or lift a spoon to his lips: "Live fully."

As a boy, I would sit next to my father as he picked up a piece of typing paper, made a few folds here and there, and then grabbed scissors. He cut a bit to the left and then turned the paper and cut a bit to the right until he created the wings and tail of an airplane.

He would bend the wings, which looked a bit like the wings of a swan. After he adjusted the ailerons, he and I stepped out into the yard. Dad pulled his long right arm back over his broad shoulder and tossed the paper plane into the air. It sailed upward, over the irises, turned and gently floated back into my outstretched hands. "You need to balance the wings for it to fly properly," he said. I held the plane as if it was a magical creature.

My father was a voracious reader: poetry, philosophy, French novels, nonfiction books on Russian icons, biographies of Rasputin and Roosevelt, the Boer Wars, plays by Molière, books on religion, art, music, the climate, tigers, and health. His study was lined with books.

When I was eighteen, I stepped out of his car to board the bus that would take me to my first year of university. As I lifted my suitcase, my father looked at me and said, "Don't let college interfere with your education, and read everything." He was a lawyer, college professor, author, and tennis player, and he loved to build things out of wood: weaving looms, stairs for our cabin in Canada, wood swords for my brothers and me, the kitchen table, and sailboats.

He gave me sailing lessons as he and I sat on the deck of the *Sea Kitten*, an eight-foot sailboat he had built in the basement. Once we were floating on the lake in Canada during a particularly windy afternoon. As I pulled on the jib, the mainsail billowed with angry air, and the boat began to tip wildly. I felt out of control, not knowing what to do. My father said gently, "If you are ever in a panic, just let go of the sails and the boat will upright itself."

I let go. The sailboat wobbled a bit and was suddenly at ease in the water, bobbing gracefully with the wind and waves.

What do I say to teenagers after my forty-year career in education? Balance your wings, read everything, if you are ever in a panic, let go of the sails . . . and live fully.

« »

When I am afraid, I will call out your name.
When I am weak, I shall reach for your hand.
Lord, Father, grant me courage and strength
so that I may live according to your plans.

19

Death

So Elmer Fudd says to Bugs Bunny (who is dressed as a game warden), "Oh, Mr. Game Warden. I hope you can help me. I've been told I could shoot wabbits and goats and pigeons and mongooses and dirty skunks and ducks. Could you tell me what season it is?"

Bugs Bunny, under his game warden's hat and wearing a red mustache for disguise, says with sly authority, "Why, certainly, me boy. It's baseball season!"

Even wily Bugs tries to deflect death, that universal moment that sits between what it is that we know for sure and what it is that defies explanation except in the context of faith.

For many years during my childhood, my grandmother spent the summer with us. She arrived from Belgium in the early spring and left at the end of October. She left behind a closet of her dresses and shoes and the aroma of her distinctive perfume that permeated the empty bedroom for the entire time that she was gone.

It's been more than thirty years since my grandmother died, and there is still in that closet a pair of her shoes. She always believed that the next summer was coming, that she would return and simply slip her feet into her summer shoes and walk downstairs and join us for breakfast.

Each July Roe and I drive to southern Ontario, Canada, to spend two weeks in a small, primitive cabin that sits beside a beautiful, meandering river.

This past July, during our first night, we heard a mouse downstairs feasting on what ended up being the contents of the cereal box that the mouse had knocked over. The following night I set up the Havahart trap that cleverly ensnares mice without killing them. (I recognize that many people laugh at my resistance to killing a mouse, but I felt that the mouse deserved another day. I am, after all, a big fan of Stuart Little and Beatrix Potter's mice.) I caught the mouse, drove two miles from the cabin, and released the brown creature into the woods—and felt satisfied that I had contributed, in a small way, to the temporary deflection of death.

The next morning, while Roe was drying her hair, she called out to me. "What is that on the floor?" There, wiggling on the bathroom tiles, was a newborn mouse. Its eyes were still closed. It had no fur. And I knew what that meant. There was a nest nearby.

I looked under the baseboard. No mice. I looked in the cabinet drawers. No mice. I pulled a box of tissues from a cubbyhole on the shelves, and there they were: five newly born gray and pink creatures wiggling and squirming. And I had tossed their mother into the woods two miles away the day before.

I didn't know what to do. I couldn't raise them, or keep them, or run back into the woods and find the mother and apologize for disrupting her family. I couldn't drown the small animals, so I scooped up the mice and the nest into a shoebox, drove two miles to the spot where I had released the mother, and heaved the nest into the woods pretending that Mrs. Tittlemouse would surely come across her children as she stepped out from under a mushroom with a basket of food in the crook of her arm.

We live at the edge of our own deaths with faith as a protective shield. Some people fear death. Some live joyfully because we believe, as the poet Mary Oliver wrote in her poem "Heron Rises from the Dark, Summer Pond," "How unlikely it is that death is a hole in the ground." Most of us do not think of our own dying; rather, we wake in the morning to consider the day's challenges, occupy ourselves with those we love, make soup, read the newspaper, endure the heat, reconsider the past, and make plans for Saturday night.

I am home now, back to the routines of living. The vacation is once again packed away in the attic and in the photographs and memories of another July that disappeared into the haze and heat.

I tried to preserve life in the salvation of a single, small mouse, and in the end I killed six others. My grandmother hugged me each time at the airport and assured me, through her tears, and deflecting the obvious, that she would see me next summer. I liked the aroma of her perfume.

"You can't catch me," said the little girl to the Atlantic Ocean as the waves tried to grab her legs and pull her into the riptide.

What season is this? Deer season? Bear season? Rabbit season?

It's baseball season! Death is inevitable, often tragic, often peaceful. In the meantime, go to the stadium and buy a hotdog.

« »
I celebrate this day of life,
while I hold on with joy
my season ticket
to the kingdom of heaven.

20

The Center Will Hold

He is before all things, and in him all things hold together.
—Colossians 1:17

In 1992, when our daughter Karen was nine years old, Derek Jeter joined the Yankees. At the time, Roe and I were Mets fans because five years earlier our oldest son, David, had latched on to David Cone's pitching.

David knew all the players, their statistics, the rules of the game. And then Derek Jeter walked into Major League baseball, and nine-year-old Karen fell in love, so we all became Yankee fans. By then David was more interested in music.

We live in Pompton Plains, New Jersey, and when I told Karen that Derek Jeter was born right here in town, in the same hospital where Karen was born nine years later, she was completely hooked.

For the past nineteen years, Derek Jeter has been a part of our house: the games, the leaping plays, the World Series. Along the way, Karen graduated from elementary and middle school, played the clarinet in high school, went to the proms, and graduated from Rutgers.

So, what happened? Where is Derek Jeter going? Where is my daughter? Where is my younger self? As another Yankee great, Yogi Berra, said, "The future ain't what it used to be."

Everything seems to be falling apart. The great sphinx in Egypt is crumbling. Glaciers are melting. We've lost faith in our politicians, banks, and churches. We live in the twenty-first century, and yet we still have countries invading countries, tribes killing tribes, one religion suppressing another, one ideology trying to outspend the other. Karen's bedroom is empty. Derek Jeter is retiring. I have gray hair.

The poet William Butler Yeats wrote in his most famous poem, "The Second Coming," "Things fall apart; the centre cannot hold." For many years, my center was my three children and Roe, the daily routines of getting up at 5:30, going to work, coming home in the evening, reading to the children, sitting on the edge of each of their beds at bedtime and listening to them tell me something interesting that happened in the day.

Yeats wrote in that same gem of a poem about anarchy loose upon the world. He spoke about innocence drowning, about the lack of conviction, and how we as a civilization have lost passionate intensity.

Yeats said that surely there must be some revelations at hand, a return to essentials. I think those essentials are all about the care for the weakest among us, the rejection of greed, the trust in self and in others, and a love of God.

But then Yeats spoke about the wasted desert sand and how darkness drops all around us. Look at the number of murders in television dramas each night and in the news.

When the falcon can no longer hear the falconer, Yeats suggests, the bird is lost, and all disappears.

Roe and I walk three, sometimes four times a week, and most of the time we walk right past the old hospital where Karen and Derek were born. The building has been converted into condominiums.

We like to talk about the day, about the news, about our three grown children, and how all our lives have changed these past twenty years.

Yesterday, as we walked past the old hospital, I saw on the cracked sidewalk the arm of Mickey Mouse. It was obviously the appendage of a Mickey Mouse plush toy. It had the familiar puffy white hand attached to a black arm. "Now who would tear off the arm of Mickey Mouse?" I asked Roe.

The Roman Empire disintegrated in the fourth and fifth centuries. Some historians suggest that the Roman military collapsed; others blame the weak economy. Many histories blame corruption in the institutions during the time of barbaric invasions of the empire.

Sidewalks crack. Daughters grow up and leave home. Fathers grow old. Mickey Mouse was pulled apart. Things change.

I wish Derek Jeter had never retired from the Yankees.

《 》

God, help us continue to maintain the center of what is important.
Help us hold together what is true and enduring:
family, honor, patience, empathy, faith, goodness. You.

21

Joy

Weeping may endure for a night,
But joy comes in the morning.
—Psalm 30:5, NKJV

I have a recurring dream. Is it death beckoning? Fear of change? Fear of retirement? A large dark mass, like a whale or the entire night sky, envelops me, and then I disappear. Each time, when I struggle to release myself from whatever it is that surrounds me, I wake up relieved that I am in my bedroom. What is the darkness that tries to grab hold of us in our imagination?

The first time I saw the nine turkeys in my mother's backyard, I was reminded of that awful dream. A wild turkey roosting for the night in a bare tree looks like something out of a horror movie. The birds were perched in the single tree, branch to branch. Their shoulders looked hunched. They were dark masses, creatures from a pirate's lagoon, perhaps. Wild turkeys can weigh up to thirty pounds, and at dusk they looked like old, frightening men in judicial robes peering down at me, judging me, wanting to creep into my dreams at night and peck at my heart. I have a suspicion about what they represent.

The very first time I saw the shadow of death was watching the 1939 movie *The Wizard of Oz*. I was a boy of ten and not prepared for those flying monkeys. The image of their silhouettes in the sky made me close the blinds in my bedroom for many years. I was startled that something could, with impunity, swoop down and grab Dorothy, Toto—or me. Being kidnapped and carried off to a dark castle frightened me. The thought of those monkeys touching me, pulling me into the air, and carrying me off left a lasting impression on me.

When many years later I read the Greek myth about Icarus, and saw the boy flying so close to the sun that the wax attaching the feathers to his arms melted, the Oz monkeys jumped into my mind. Of course, Icarus plunged to his death.

I wish life could be as simple as not flying too close to the sun.

Grandfather Clock in Captain Kangaroo's Treasure House also frightened me. I didn't like his voice or the way his eyes blinked at me when he woke up. I disliked the eyes in *The Great Gatsby* on the billboard of the oculist Dr. T.J. Eckleburg, all-knowing eyes keeping track of Gatsby, Daisy, Nick, and Tom Buchanan—and me—as we all plunged forward into the confusion of our lives that, as the novel suggested, ended in death just the same.

I don't want to die. I don't want to be swallowed up by a dark mass. I don't want to be dragged up into the air by flying monkeys. I don't want talking clocks and billboards haunting me with their smug visions.

Last summer, Roe and I took a hike in the Canadian woods not far from the small cabin my father built fifty years ago. The underbrush was thick, and the ground was soft and moist. Suddenly I tripped over an exposed root and fell forward, my chest hitting the ground forcefully. Roe quickly asked if I was okay. "Yes," I gasped, for the fall had knocked the wind out of me. When I sat up, I looked to my left and saw, inches from where my chest had landed, a sharp spike. It was the broken remains of a small tree trunk, like a dagger protruding up from the ground. If I had fallen just a few inches to my left, I would have been stabbed in the heart. It is the closest I have ever come to dying.

I think about that spike often, or the sword, or the cancer, or the pneumonia, or old age, the eventual stab in the heart. Something will carry us away into the darkness, but this afternoon I will cut the grass or vacuum the living room.

I do not plan to die today.

« »

Lord, protect me from fear, protect me from anxiety;
remind me that you are waiting for me at the end of my earthly life.

22

Secrets

There is a river whose streams make glad the city of God,
the holy place where the Most High dwells.
—Psalm 46:4

He looked official in his dark uniform. As our car inched its way to the Canadian border, Roe handed me our passports. When the car ahead of us drove off, the border guard leaned out of his booth and waved me forward.

"What is the purpose of your visit?" he asked as I handed him the passports.

"Our two weeks' vacation."

"Where are you going?" He scanned our passports into a machine.

"Combermere, Ontario. We have a small cabin."

"Are you bringing in any firearms?" the man asked as he returned the passports.

"No," I said. "Just our clothes and some food."

He looked at me. I looked at him, and then he smiled and said, "Welcome to Canada."

As Roe and I drove across the Thousand Island Bridge at the St. Lawrence Seaway, I pointed out the first Canadian flag that I saw in full exposure at the top of a pole just to the right of the highway. We agreed that the Canadian flag is one of the prettiest in the world with that bold red maple leaf.

Ever since I was seven years old, I have made the 500-mile trip to our one-room cabin on the Madawaska River three hours west of Ottawa, and four hours east of Toronto—for two weeks every summer.

Now that I am sixty-seven, I feel more and more like Ernest Hemingway whenever I make this trip to the wide, meandering river: rugged, confident, thinking I ought to grow a beard and write about rattlesnakes and giant bears.

While everyone in my family will attest that I am hopeless with engines and mechanical things, and that I tolerate the motorboat, it is in the canoe where I feel that I am truly in Canada. I enjoy the serenity of the river that is often completely empty except for the Canadian ambassadors. In late June and early July, the loons are nurturing their young, usually one or two chicks that can already swim. This is the only time of the year when anyone can slowly glide in a boat right up to the mother loon and admire her beauty. She won't dive and disappear because she is protecting her chicks.

I know Vermont and Maine claim the loons as their own, but I cannot help but believe all loons are really Canadians. And yes, there is nothing more mystical then hearing the cry of the loon in the early morning as the mist rises from the river.

Henry David Thoreau had it right:

In the middle of the night, as indeed each time that we lay on the shore of a lake, we heard the voice of the loon, loud and distinct, from far over the lake. It is a very wild sound, quite in keeping with the place and the circumstances of the traveler, and very unlike the voice of a bird. I could lie awake for hours listening to it, it is so thrilling.

This year, while paddling downriver to the small village for the morning newspaper, I saw a sparrow in the water flapping its wings in an exhaustive attempt to escape from the water. In a few more moments, the bird surely would have drowned.

I pushed the canoe hard in the water with my paddle and quickly eased beside the helpless bird. I scooped it up into my hands, placed it on my lap, and quickly paddled to the riverbank. I felt like St. Francis as I walked to the shore, opened my cupped hands, and watched the sparrow fly up in sudden realization that it was free. As the bird disappeared over a clump of pine trees, I thought about Langston Hughes's quote: "Hold fast to dreams, for if dreams die, life is a broken-winged bird that cannot fly."

When I returned to my boat and headed for town, a blue heron, in graceful ease of long wings and neck, flew over me in the distant sky. A turtle slid off a wet log as the waves from my boat pushed toward the shore. And to the left, a beaver made its own little waves, and there a dragonfly zoomed alongside my canoe. I felt compelled to tip my Yankee baseball cap to it, but the insect shot off to the left and disappeared.

There is a quote in Kenneth Grahame's book *The Wind in the Willows* where Ratty says, "Believe me, my young friend, there is nothing—absolutely nothing—half so much worth doing as simply messing about in boats."

And it is worth crossing the Canadian border, breathing in the Canadian air, visiting the loons, messing about in boats, and accepting for a brief few days the secrets from the river.

Hermann Hesse wrote in his little book *Siddhartha,*

> There is no such thing as time. . . . The river is everywhere at the same time, at the source and at the mouth, at the waterfall, at the ferry, at the current, in the ocean and in the mountains, everywhere, and that the present only exists for it, not the shadow of the past, nor the shadow of the future.

《 》

Let us carry with us each day the secrets of the river.

23

Continuity

Jesus Christ is the same yesterday and today and forever.
—Hebrews 13:8

Recently my wife and I discovered a leak in the small showerhead in the bathroom, and when the plumber arrived, he said it had to be replaced. "What would you like?" he asked. I said that he could install whatever he thought best.

When the plumber left, Roe and I stepped into the bathroom, pulled back the shower curtain, and both were disappointed. The new showerhead looked huge, out of place, not what we were accustomed to seeing. It looked like a fat glob of chrome with too many holes, as if it had been pierced with the back of a steel porcupine.

After a week or so, I said to my wife, "That new showerhead looks good after all." She agreed.

We all seem to thrive on what is familiar, but then time soothes us, and we release the shadows of the past and accept the shapes and reality of what is new. But there are some things that will never dissolve in our hearts.

It is reassuring to stand in New Jersey's Liberty Park and look across the Hudson at One World Trade Center, yet it is also filled with our continued national sorrow at what seemed to be the beginning of international, hateful killings in the name of religion.

Driving from New Jersey to Kennedy Airport and seeing the stainless steel globe of the 1964–65 World's Fair in Flushing brings me great delight each time I see it, reminding me of my thirteen-year-old self walking through the General Motors pavilion or seeing the Pietà at the Vatican pavilion. But I also harbor a consistent sorrow that the fair no longer exists and I am no longer a thirteen-year-old boy.

My family and I just returned from our annual two-week vacation in Ontario, staying at the family cabin in the quaint town I have returned to again and again for the past sixty years, and nothing appears to change in this small Brigadoon of my life.

We buy the same ice-cream cones in the same wood-floored grocery store. We canoe on the same river that has not changed course. We listen to the same loons, roast the same marshmallows, and look up at the same stars and Milky Way. We walk among the same wildflowers: black-eyed Susans, buttercups, Queen Anne's lace, milkweed. We see the same blue herons, monarch butterflies, ducks, and sunsets. We gather the same wild blueberries and raspberries.

During the fifth day of our vacation, it rained, and I was looking for something to do in the cabin, so I walked over to the bookshelf filled with old magazines, novels, an atlas, games, and a thick book with a straightforward title: *Crossword Puzzles*.

In the United States, every day, approximately 50 million people do crossword puzzles. It is interesting to note that the crossword puzzle has a short history, having been created for the first time by journalist Arthur Wynne on December 21, 1913, for John Pulitzer's now-defunct *New York World* newspaper.

When I opened the crossword puzzle book and randomly came across a nearly finished puzzle, I noticed my father's handwriting. My father—a writer, professor, and word master, died at the age of 100. He knew Greek, Latin, French, history, philosophy, and architecture, but he didn't know the answer to one of the puzzle's clues: trout basket.

For a second my father was alive as he and I struggled to figure out the answer. He had the first letter "C" from a horizontal word, and in the third space the letter "E," but not the rest.

I knew the answer because I remembered one of my favorite lines from David Guterson's collection of short stories about the Pacific Northwest: "In my dream I had enough to do, filling my creel with silver trout."

"Dad," I almost said aloud, "Creel. The answer is 'creel.' It's that small wicker basket fishermen use to hold the caught fish."

I looked up from the crossword puzzle book. "Dad?"

« »

In the name of the Father, I seek what is forever.
In the name of the Son, I recognize what will never leave me.
In the name of the Holy Spirit, I dwell inside what is eternal.

24

The Praying Mantis

And God said, "Let there be light," and there was light.
—Genesis 1:3

August is like a secret playland for a boy with an imagination and a disdain for school. I was that boy when I was ten, a boy born as a baby boomer, immune to humidity and eager to chase as many adventures as possible, knowing that summer would inevitably end and I would once again be confined to a cold September school desk.

The morning of the praying mantis began with my usual mug of Ovaltine and a glass of orange juice. I checked my pocket for my magnifying glass, my piece of Bazooka bubblegum, my dime-sized compass, and the dollar I always kept in case the ice-cream truck drove by. (It never did.)

The house I grew up in was a three-story American four-square, sided with cedar shingles and filled with the clamor of my five brothers and sisters, the aroma of my mother's baking bread, and the sound of my father rustling the newspaper.

Mine was an ordinary American childhood blessed with the victory of World War II. Both my parents cheered the American and British troops as they were liberated from Nazi occupation in Belgium in 1945. I was born in the heart of the baby boom in the stability of financial security, in a house filled with books, and with parents who left my sisters and brothers and me with the freedom to read, play, and imagine as we chose during those hot, memorable summers of so long ago.

After breakfast it was my habit to grab my Davy Crockett coonskin cap and rush outside to see what I could find: a frog in the small pond at the edge of the woods, a salamander under the rocks along the summer stream, a bird's nest in the mock orange bushes.

I developed an early affection for animals and bugs. I felt like James Henry Trotter in Roald Dahl's famous book *James and the Giant Peach*. James enjoyed his adventures with a grasshopper, centipede, and earthworm. Mine began with the praying mantis.

I had never seen a praying mantis before, and as I walked past the rhododendron bushes and stared in the direction of the large rock that looked like the back of a giant turtle, I saw what appeared to be a grasshopper, but of course the closer I walked toward the creature, the bigger it seemed to grow. To my surprise, when I leaned down, the insect didn't jump away but stood on its four legs, then reared up in a motionless position that did indeed look like a creature at prayer.

I pulled out my plastic magnifying glass, closed one eye as all good boy scientists do, and examined my newfound . . . *monster*! Along with the antennas on its head, it had two horrifying eyes that were wide apart like a space creature from the movie screen. It had two ugly spiked arms. Its lower body looked like a fierce hornet.

I felt like brave Davy Crockett until the bug suddenly sprang up at me. I didn't know it had wings. I didn't know it could fly. I didn't know if the praying mantis could inject poisonous venom into the neck of a fraudulent mountain man, king of the wild frontier.

I ran back past the rhododendrons, waving my arms above my head, hoping to beat away what I imagined to be Rodan, the famous giant flying monster in the iconic Japanese movie.

In a panic I told my father what I had found, and he gave me a small paperback book on insects, sat down with me on the couch, and read aloud the attributes of the praying mantis. I learned that they eat bugs (and their own mates) but not ten-year-old boys.

When I told my mother about this giant insect I had found in the yard, she told me that in Africa it was considered long ago to be a god. The word *mantis* is from the Greek word meaning "prophet."

When I tried to convince my brothers that I had found a dragon, they looked at me and laughed.

August for me long ago was a time for children to sit on the back porch and spit out watermelon seeds, a time to swim, build tree forts, play stickball, climb trees, and hunt for frogs. But then, as the rock group The Byrds' song "Turn! Turn! Turn!" says, the calendar quickly turned to reveal the month of September. I was back in school, learning about fractions, diagramming sentences, and being forced to twist my penmanship into the standard stilted loops of the Palmer Method. The boy was suddenly shackled to a desk, then the boy became a man, and the man still imagines what it might have been like if he had hopped onto the back of the praying mantis as it whirred up into the magical air of August heat.

« »

Guide me, Lord, to be childlike again:
to sing, lick Popsicles, laugh.
Guide me to the playfield of what I remember.

25

Heat

As long as the earth endures, seedtime and harvest,
cold and heat, summer and winter,
day and night will never cease.
—Genesis 8:22

Those of us of a certain age remember what it was like to grow up without air conditioning. The air conditioner was invented in the early 1900s, but it was too expensive to buy during the early boomer years. Do you remember the first air conditioner in your home, or in your father's car? But somehow, a summer without air conditioning gave us baby boomers more reasons to use our imaginations to beat the heat.

The summer heat was like a twisting dragon curling down from the sky, weaving into our lives with its hot breath and relentless power. We did all that we could to battle the heat and humidity that made our doors expand, that squeezed moisture from our skin, and that compelled the cicadas to crackle at the tops of trees.

My sister Anne and I made pitchers of Kool-Aid, pressing our cold glasses against our cheeks before drinking the sweet, colored water. We fished out quarters from the couch and from my father's winter coats in search of just enough money to stop the ice-cream truck and buy a Popsicle or creamsicle.

Over two thousand years ago the Romans referred to the hot summer days as the dog days because this phenomenon coincided with the appearance in the low night sky of Sirius, the dog star, in the Canis Major constellation—the brightest star in the sky.

Harper Lee, in her novel *To Kill a Mockingbird*, wrote about the heat in the little southern town of Maycomb. "Somehow, it was hotter then. . . . Men's stiff collars wilted by nine in the morning. Ladies bathed before noon, after their three o'clock naps, and by nightfall were like soft teacakes with frostings of sweat and sweet talcum."

I remember the smell of road tar in the heat and the wet cloth my grandmother draped around her neck as she sat on the porch and fanned herself with the folded July newspaper.

It was cool inside the railroad underpass. I'd stick my head in the freezer now and again, making sure my grandmother was in the next room for she was convinced, when she caught me once, that I would freeze my brain.

One of the best places to keep cool in the summer was in the center of the mock orange bushes that grew wild in the side lot of our house. Anne and I took garden shears and made our way into the bushes, cutting away the inside sticks and leaves until we created a summer igloo. We sat on the ground. The earth was moist. We were in the shade. I liked looking out into the garden from our little house and seeing the daylilies nearly glow in the hot summer light.

While the world seemed to stand still in the hot days of July, Anne and I hopped on our bicycles with towels around our necks and headed for the town pool: shallow on one side and deep on the other. To the right, water gushed from the filtration system's pipe, to the left the shade of the maple tree where mothers sat with their babies in carriages as the "big" kids held their noses and bobbed underwater.

It was here that Anne and I swam like otters between each other's legs and where we balanced ourselves underwater on our hands, sticking our legs straight up into the air. It was here we pretended that we were Olympic swimmers. The water was cool, the air fresh. The horrible monster heat was reduced to a soothing massage against our cool bodies as we stretched out on our blankets on the soft summer grass.

Roe and I, now in our sixties, decided it was time to install central air conditioning in our little house. When the work was complete and the installers left, we stood sheepishly before our small control panel, adjusted the temperature to 78, and listened as the quiet machine in the attic clinked on and cool air began to stream out of the small ceiling vents that were cut into each room.

While I marvel at the technology and am grateful for the mechanical slayer of the heat dragon, the new air-conditioning system doesn't seem to satisfy me as much as sitting inside the mock orange bush with my sister, or swimming with her in the cool, dreamy place of our childhood when the sun was hot and our laughter cool and easy.

« »

Let us sleep in comfort, let us sleep in peace.
Let us stretch under the coolness of the shade tree
and under the shadow and comfort of God.

26

Home

Then they all went home.
—John 7:53

As we grow older, we start thinking about "the way things used to be," and we just want to go home.

A family friend who was a surgeon said that often when patients were dying, they would call out for their mothers. In my mother's old age, she liked to talk about her home in Belgium: her childhood bedroom, the greenhouse out back, her mother's pea soup.

In Robert Frost's poem "The Death of the Hired Man," he wrote that "Home is the place where, when you have to go there, they have to take you in."

The American writer Thornton Wilder wrote the play *Our Town*. It was first performed in Princeton, New Jersey, on January 22, 1938, and it won the Pulitzer Prize that same year. It's a little play about a place called Grover's Corners up in New Hampshire, a little play that reminds us what is important: the ordinary day, our neighbors and a bit of gossip, the people buried in the cemetery, and the sound of children walking home from school.

We still believe in the American town, a nice place for a Memorial Day parade with the fire engines and the Girl Scouts tossing candy, a place for a pancake breakfast over at the church hall, fireworks at the ball field on the Fourth of July, people waking up expecting coffee, or the sound of the distant train passing through on the way to Buffalo or Chicago.

Some people might complain that the only thing to do in a small town is go look at the canon in the park.

Pompton Plains, New Jersey, where I've lived for decades, had a railroad station once. Kids walk to school. Everyone knows the police officers by their first names. Robbie Jones's grandfather opened the hardware store in April 1929. The building has stood there since 1818. I can remember buying grass seed there and Robbie asking about my three children by name. When I walked out of the store, a neighbor was bending over the seed rack looking for zinnias. A small town is all about planting zinnias.

Jones Hardware was on the front cover of *The New Yorker* magazine on May 7, 1966. The famous illustrator Arthur Getz drew many covers for that publication, and he saw the charm and simplicity of the bags of peat moss and rakes for sale out front letting people know that the store was open for business.

There's a plaque outside the middle school that reads "King Louis XVI's French Army under the command of General Count de Rochambeau camped here on the Mandeville farm in August 1781." The story goes that even George Washington rode with his soldiers down the main street. There are eight Revolutionary War soldiers buried in the only cemetery in town. During the Civil War, Pompton Plains was a stop on the Underground Railroad, the secret route for southern slaves seeking freedom in the northern states and Canada.

In Pompton Plains, it seems that everyone believes a groundhog lives under their shed.

S.L.M. Barlow is quoted as saying of composer Aaron Copland's "Appalachian Spring," "Here were the tart herbs of plain American speech, the pasture, without the flowers of elocution, . . . the clean rhythms, . . . the irony and the homespun tenderness." Small-town America is all about plain speech and homespun tenderness.

Doug McKeon, the actor who played the disgruntled boy beside the disgruntled old man in the film *On Golden Pond*, was born in Pompton Plains. He played Billy Ray, a disillusioned teenage boy, and he said in the film to Norman Thayer, played by Henry Fonda, "So, I heard you turned eighty today."

Grumpy Norman answered, "Is that what you heard?"

"Yeah. Man, that's really old."

"You should meet my father," Norman scowled.

"Your father's still alive?"

"No, but you should meet him," Norman says with a homespun, deadpan voice that the boy clearly understood.

President Jimmy Carter, always proud to live in small-town America, lives on Woodland Drive in Plains, Georgia. I live on Woodland Court in Pompton Plains, New Jersey. It's a small town of 16,000 people. The pizza is good, the children read *To Kill a Mockingbird* over at the high school, and each year Santa Claus (Robbie Jones) rides on the back of the fire truck, visiting the homes of children.

Derek Jeter was born here in Pompton Plains on June 26, 1974. He is quoted as saying, "I like to dance and sing when there's no one around, but, if I'm out, I'm really shy about it. So it takes a lot to get me going, but I enjoy being around music."

A hometown is all about main streets and the courage to sing and live in homespun tenderness. I can still hear Robbie Jones' kind voice as he speaks about his father and grandfather working in the hardware store.

Emily Webb in *Our Town* calls out, "Does anyone ever realize life while they live it . . . every, every minute?" At which the Stage Manager says with resignation, "No. Saints and poets maybe . . . they do some."

I believe America is one local town and we are all mostly saints and poets who realize life as we live it and recognize how grand it is to lean over and select a pack of zinnia seeds in the spring at Jones Hardware.

« »

I remember the home of my parents.
I remember the home of my wife.
Remind me today, God, of the open comforts of your home:
compassion, forgiveness, love.

AUTUMN

Season of mists and mellow fruitfulness

—John Keats

27

Clap Your Hands

O clap your hands, all peoples; Shout to God with the voice of joy.
—Psalm 47:1, NASB

There is evidence that Jersey City, New Jersey, has one of the highest concentrations of artists in the country. Walter Dean Myers, a prolific writer of engaging young adult literature, lived here. Nathan Lane, one of America's funniest and most accomplished Broadway actors, was born in Jersey City. While Frank Sinatra was born next door in Hoboken, he lived for many years in Jersey City as he honed his destiny as one of our most endearing crooners of the twentieth and twenty-first centuries. Comedian Flip Wilson was also born in the city that has been called America's golden door as host to Ellis Island.

Yes, Jersey City has claims to movie stars, musicians, authors, engravers, painters, and it was the home of Richie Havens.

I did not know who Richie Havens was in 1969, and I barely knew who *I* was in 1969, a shy, guarded boy who liked girls, envied the guy with a Ford Mustang, and hadn't a clue about any world beyond high school and Friday nights at the drive-in movie theater.

In the early weeks of August 1969 I was playing basketball with some of my friends. We had just graduated from high school. Bobby O'Reilly, one of my best friends in high school, said that he heard there was some sort of a concert starting in a few days in upstate New York. "Anyone interested in going?"

We bounced the ball, passed, shot, dribbled. No one was interested. I distinctly remember saying, "Who wants to go to some crummy outdoor concert?"

Needless to say, that "crummy outdoor concert" became the most iconic symbol of the sixties generation and defined the way we looked at ourselves as

Americans and as people of hope. Baby boomers have a right to claim Woodstock as their own.

It was Richie Havens who opened the Woodstock festival on August 18, 1969, and when I heard his song "Freedom" on the radio for the first time, something stirred inside of me that I didn't even know existed. I am a baby boomer, but I was a late bloomer to the swell of change and hope our generation developed.

In 1969, I was more excited about the release of the first Led Zeppelin album than I was that Richard Nixon became the thirty-seventh president of the United States. I remember seeing on television the first Boeing 747 and yawning, and I had great fun at a pool party on July 20 as we watched Neil Armstrong place his foot on the moon. I was more interested in Susan and my potato chips than in that giant leap for mankind.

And I remember a few days earlier some vague story about Senator Kennedy at some place called Chappaquiddick.

And then I heard Richie Havens on the radio. The way his deep voice resonated, the way he attacked the guitar strings, the way he called out the word "freedom" stirred me. He sang in a plaintive manner that he felt like a motherless child, that he felt almost gone, that he felt a long way from his home. He called out words to us all, saying we need our mothers and our brothers, and then he asked that we all clap hands together. "Clap hands! Clap hands! Hey, yeah!"

I loved that song and all that Richie Havens represented on that day in 1969. His voice was the beginning of my own journey toward an awareness of life that I'd never experienced. I became an English major in college, and then I slowly discovered *Hamlet*: "This above all: to thine own self be true, and it must follow, as the night the day, thou canst not then be false to any man." I heard Scout whispering in *To Kill a Mockingbird*: "Atticus, he was real nice," to which the father says, "Most people are, Scout, when you finally see them."

Many baby boomers discovered portals to a deeper understanding of the world. For some it was a line in a book of poetry; for others advice from a father or teacher. For me, on some level, my leap into Alice in Wonderland's rabbit hole, my full embrace of the baby boomer's flag and peace symbol began with Richie Havens's plea for freedom, for comfort, for home, and for love.

Richie Havens died on April 22, 2013, and at his family's request his ashes were scattered on the famous site on August 18, forty-four years after his chanting for freedom to more than 400,000 young people. His voice helped me become more aware of what is truly important in this sometimes-sorry world.

"Art," the painter Edgar Degas wrote, "is not what you see, but what you make others see." Richie Havens, resident of Jersey City, New Jersey, resident of the world, helped millions of people see the power of freedom and the path to self-discovery.

Clap your hands. Clap your hands. Clap your hands. Hey . . . yeah.

« »

Freedom. Freedom. Freedom.
God sings the lyrics of my freedom.

28

Excelsior

And when his time of service was ended, he went to his home.
—Luke 1:23, ESV

Students and teachers across the country are returning to school, and I am sitting home wondering if I did the right thing. One year has passed since I retired as an English department supervisor after a long career in education. On my last day, I was given a helium balloon with colorful words printed on its surface: Happy Retirement.

After the hugs and goodbyes, everyone went home for the summer, but I walked back to my office for the last time, holding my balloon by the string as it followed behind me.

When I stepped into my office, I looked at the empty shelves and at the bare desk where I had sat through many seasons. I looked at the silent phone and at the empty worktables. As I sat at my desk feeling one more time like a serious school administrator, I pulled out a piece of typing paper from my silent computer printer and reached into the top desk drawer for a pen.

I held the pen firmly in my right hand and wrote in bold letters on the white paper *EXCELSIOR*, the Latin word that means "ever higher." The poet Henry Wadsworth Longfellow highlighted the word in his poem about a young man who courageously climbed over a winter mountain pass with a banner that read *Excelsior*. Even though he was warned of the danger, he felt he had to go on with his life's journey. He left his village behind in the winter storm as his lover begged, "Oh stay, and rest thy weary head upon this breast!"

The poem's last stanza reveals the young man's fate:

There in the twilight cold and gray,
Lifeless, but beautiful, he lay,
And from the sky, serene and far,
A voice fell like a falling star,
    Excelsior!

I returned the pen to the drawer, leaving it behind for the next person who would take over my desk, my room, and my school. Would he or she see my fading shadow? I folded my own little banner three times.

Walt Whitman wrote in his own poem titled "Excelsior":

And who has receiv'd the love of the most friends? for I know what it
    is to receive the passionate love of many friends

I was leaving behind a staff of teachers I had hired, admired, and loved. I was leaving behind children looking for compassion and corroboration that they were okay. I felt like Ebenezer Scrooge looking back at the ghosts of my past life as I sat in my office alone in a building that holds more than 4,000 people on an ordinary school day.

I grabbed the string on my balloon. The balloon tipped gently toward me. I tied my little message to the balloon, and then I walked to the open window behind my desk.

In that wonderful book by Jules Verne, *Around the World in Eighty Days*, Phileas Fogg was asked about his ridiculous impending adventure in a balloon, "Monsieur is going to leave home?" Phileas answered with a quick, brave, simple response: "We are going round the world."

I held the balloon out the window with my note, and then I released it into the open air. I was able to watch it rise over the building, over the trees, higher and higher until an upper wind pushed it north and it disappeared out of view.

I loved working with students and teachers. I loved creating a curriculum of novels for the children to read. I liked advising young people about their future choices. I delighted in being in the presence of teenagers who were filled with optimism and fears, humor and grumpiness.

On the last day of school, I watched the students depart in school buses. I watched my teachers walk down the hall and out the door on their way to their summer vacations and to their waiting lives.

When a job is complete, when a career comes to an end, what do we feel? What person did we help? What difference did we make in the world? I locked my window and walked out of my office. I stood in the hallway and firmly held the doorknob. As I slowly closed the door for the last time, I listened to the final click as it snugly fit into its solid frame. I went around the world of books and children these past forty years. I will miss the adventure.

To the teachers and students entering the classrooms this September I say, "Read, listen, think, and love. Know there is a beginning and an end. What you do in the middle is what counts. Excelsior."

« »

For the work you have given me, I praise you Lord;
for the fruits of my labor, I thank thee.

29

Our Potential

Many are the plans in a person's heart
but it is the Lord's purpose that prevails.
—Proverbs 19:21

Autumn is the season of humility. Leaves begin to accept their changing colors and age. The beach waters submit to the lowering temperatures. Children put away their shorts and swimsuits and accept the power the school bell has over their lives. But there is one brave element in autumn that seems to retain power and strength: the humble acorn.

When I was a boy, I sat high in an oak tree one October, knowing that my mother would soon sit at the base of her favorite tree to spend a bit of quiet time away from the noise of her six children. My mother arrived, spread a blanket, and sat in her renewed peace, but then a single acorn dropped beside her. She picked it up. Another dropped on her head. She reached up and stroked her hair. After the third falling acorn, she looked up and saw the teasing wave of my hand. She smiled and called me down beside her, her autumn boy, and she held me in an embrace that I still savor.

As I grew a bit older, I felt I was more a man than a boy, for men smoked pipes. I took an acorn, drilled a small hole with a nail, and stuck a thin stick into the hole: voilà an autumn pipe.

But like the ant or bee, often the smallest things in nature have the greatest power. Ralph Waldo Emerson wrote from his home in Concord, Massachusetts, in the late 1800s: "The creation of a thousand forests is in one acorn."

Children take twenty or thirty years to mature, but the brave acorn matures in six to twenty-four months, rich in nutrients: it contain carbohydrates, fats, and protein and is packed with vitamins B12, B6, folate, riboflavin, thiamine, calcium, phosphorus, potassium, and niacin.

To me, the acorn is a symbol for the great potential within all of us: this small package that, with the proper conditions of light and moisture, will grow into a seventy- or one hundred–foot tree and produce 2,000 acorns a year that constitute 25 percent of a deer's diet in the fall.

The playwright George Bernard Shaw wrote, "Think of the fierce energy concentrated in an acorn! You bury it in the ground, and it explodes into an oak! Bury a sheep, and nothing happens but decay."

When children go off to school this fall season, sit with them under the oak tree; place an acorn in the palm of their hands and tell them that they, like the acorn, hold great power within themselves. They, like the acorn, hold great potential, and they can grow, extend their rich minds and bodies into the forest of this sometimes dry and empty land we call reality.

Tell the children that there is much to living if we plant ourselves deeply in the soil of goodness, education, and hope for the future. Tell them that, like the humble acorn, they too will sprout roots hidden deep within themselves.

An acorn in the hand is a vibrant reminder about what we may become. Let us remind the children in our school this autumn as the astronomer Carl Sagan wrote, "This oak tree and me, we're made of the same stuff."

Each child—that humble acorn—is waiting for teachers' wisdom, a parent's hug, for life and love. We are all made of the same stuff.

« »

Many are the choices we have; many ways the roads do bend.
Lord in Heaven, guide me so that my path is lined
with clear directions to your open arms.

30

Vision

O Lord my God; Enlighten my eyes . . .
—Psalm 13:3, NKJV

When I was a boy, I was the only one in my family who didn't need glasses except for my brother who was blind, so I had a keen awareness of my eyes at a young age. I'd walk around the house pretending that I was blind, trying to understand what it was like for my brother to live in constant darkness.

When my father was out in the garden, I'd sometimes borrow his horn-rimmed glasses and adjust them on my nose as I stood before a mirror trying to look as smart as he did.

I even felt a kinship to Superman, my hero. He and I both had keen vision. I remember staring with my x-ray vision at the living room wall as I tried to see my grandmother in the kitchen darning socks. It never worked, and I envied Clark Kent with the thick, dark glasses he used as a partial disguise.

It is easy to take our vision for granted. It works like a flashlight, letting us see out of the darkness at the flip of a switch or a flip of our eyelids. The eyes seek out light and allow the brain to do its work and translate for us the images that magically appear before us.

When our children were young, Roe and I took them to a cave in Ontario, Canada, for a guided tour. At one point, as we all stood in a room filled with stalactites and stalagmites under a number of bright electric bulbs, the guide said, "Let's see what pure darkness is like when I turn off the electricity." When she clicked off the lights, there was, at first, an immediate gasp as we all recognized the helplessness we felt in the black, black environment, but then my three kids began to giggle. I looked down, and there were stripes of light jiggling close to the floor. "Hey! Look at my sneakers!" my son Michael said to his mother. We had bought my boy those sneakers with illuminated materials sewn to the sides, and sure enough, the dark cave revealed the movements of Michael's small feet as he jumped up and down for the crowd.

Over 2,000 years ago, people in old-world Egypt used polished crystal stones to magnify objects.

In grammar school I learned that Nero is said to have worn a monocle made of a polished emerald. I liked that, this emerald bulging from the eye of the emperor. Kids like bulging eyes.

In the early eleventh century, reading stones were invented, glass shaped into orbs that produced a magnification that allowed monks with poor vision to read manuscripts, and it is assumed that Salvino D'Armate of Italy invented the first eyeglasses in 1284.

One gray morning eight years ago, while I was sitting on the couch reading the morning paper, I reached for the lamp beside me because I couldn't see the newsprint. When I clicked on the lamp and returned to the paper, I was annoyed. "What is wrong with the lamp?" Within a few days I realized it wasn't the lamp; it was my eyes. I needed reading glasses. Superman doesn't need glasses. Only my brothers and sisters need glasses.

I didn't want glasses. I didn't tell Roe. I squinted at reports at work. I thought that my eyes would adjust themselves and I'd be able to see clearly again. I didn't want an emerald sticking out of my eye. I didn't want a reading stone. I didn't want to grow old.

Superman's weakness was kryptonite. Our weakness as human beings is the diminishment of our cells as they slowly work through their life cycles, moving us from the elasticity of youth to the slow fluids and weakened hearts and bones of our aging bodies.

It is now September, the beginning of the slow decline of summer's heat and the garden's beauty. Soon the trees will shed their leaves, revealing their thin skeletons. Grass will shrivel, and the cold air and early darkness will descend upon us like a shroud. I am sixty-four years old.

When I joined my mother for dinner last night, I stood beside my father's empty lounge chair and found his glasses on the table. I carried the glasses with me to the bathroom, closed the door, stood before the mirror, placed the glasses onto my nose, and I looked into the mirror through the lens of my father's glasses, and then I cried.

Dylan Thomas had it right in his poem "Do Not Go Gentle into That Good Night." "Though wise men at their end know dark is right . . . Rage, rage against the dying of the light."

« »

Blessed are the pure of heart for they shall see.

31

Rosie

But Ruth replied, "Don't urge me to leave you
or to turn back from you. Where you go
I will go, and where you stay I will stay."
—Ruth 1:16

"There was an old woman who lived in a shoe," goes the nursery rhyme. "She had so many children, she didn't know what to do." Whenever I think of these words, I remember Rosie, one of our neighbors. The next phrases do not fit her at all: "She gave them some broth without any bread, then whipped them all soundly and put them to bed."

What *does* fit? Rosie taught me this song when I was a child, and in my mind she was always old and lived in a house that was not a shoe but was still a magical place.

I would sit with Rosie in her sunporch surrounded by white and purple African violets. Rows of glass shelves covered all the wide windows, and each shelf supported rows and rows of small clay pots of flowers. "They like tea. Each day I give them a tablespoon of tea," Rosie said. Who best to offer tea to African violets but Rosie, and perhaps Alice in Wonderland.

Rosie sat in her rocking chair and told me stories about her life. "When I was a girl, I lived in New York City, the Lower East Side. Once a year we had this great picnic sponsored by our Lutheran Church, St. Mark's. That was in the spring of 1904. We were all excited because that year we were going on a boat to the picnic at Locust Point on the Long Island Sound. Then I got sick. Diphtheria. My mother said I was forbidden to go. It was one of the worst days of my life. I loved the church picnic, and to go on a boat, well that was the best part. I was so disappointed, and angry with my mother. Christopher, have you ever heard of the *General Slocum*?"

I shook my head back and forth as Rosie sat in her chair like Scheherazade, the famous Persian storyteller of *1001 Nights*.

"Well, there was a fire on the boat. There were more than 1,300 people on board, mostly women and children. Many of my friends. More than a thousand people died. The captain didn't turn towards the shore. The life jackets were rotted and useless. So many people burned to death on the boat. So many women drowned because when they jumped into the water, the heavy, fashionable clothes that they wore at the time dragged them to the bottom of the river."

Rosie also told me, "At night, when no one is looking, the house stands up on chicken legs and spins around and around until the sun rises." I liked that.

The first time I watched television was in Rosie's house. She had a small black-and-white set to the left of her front door. She rolled out a mat, where I sat and watched Whitey Ford pitching in Yankee Stadium. I thought I was looking into a miraculous crystal glass. As I watched the game with Rosie, she'd bring out a bowl of potato chips, always a bowl of potato chips from her magical kitchen.

Rosie's kitchen had the aroma of baking bread, or there'd be an apple pie cooling on the open windowsill. If I visited her in the evening, her kitchen was illuminated with a small, single bulb above the sink that gave the entire room a golden glow, a honey look to the walls, chairs, and floor. But the best part of the kitchen was the bottom drawer.

Rosie had a table in the kitchen near the basement door. The table had three drawers. The top drawer stored spoons, knives, and forks. The middle drawer is where Rosie kept her clean towels and cloth napkins, but the bottom drawer—ah! the treasure of Long John Silver.

The bottom drawer contained Milky Way bars, 3 Musketeers, Bonomo Turkish Taffy, Cracker Jack, Tootsie Rolls, Hershey's chocolate bars, Sugar Daddies, Jujyfruits. Whenever I wanted, I could open the drawer and help myself.

Rosie always opened her arms wide and called out "Christopher" when I walked up her lawn as she stood at her front door on the brick steps waiting for me.

Rosie's black and gold grandfather clock sat in the corner of the living room like a slender guard watching over me as it ticked off the seconds of my childhood.

In her dining room cabinet Rosie had a collection of wooden dolls and figures her son sent to her during his time in the Korean War. "Now, Christopher, if you put a nickel on the head of the fat little man on the bottom shelf, it will bring you good luck." Rosie gave me a nickel, and I faithfully balanced the gray coin on the head of this small, wooden man with his legs crossed and a happy smile painted on his face.

Rosie's husband had died young. Her sons had cancer. Rosie had cancer. I didn't know all this back then. Rosie let me be a child with a happy smile painted on my face. She was my good luck. Children need to be protected from sorrow and ugliness so that they can develop a solid foundation in fantasy, heroes, magic, and awe.

Decades after her death, I still drive by Rosie's old house every now and then. To most people it is just a house, but if I look close enough, the house might turn into a shoe, or stand up on its chicken legs and spin around and around, then quickly return to its foundation and smile.

I smile back.

« »

Let us seek the face of God in those who love us.

32

Autumn

*Be patient, therefore, brothers, until the coming of the Lord. See how the
farmer waits for the precious fruit of the earth, being patient about it,
until it receives the early and the late rains. You also, be patient. Establish
your hearts, for the coming of the Lord is at hand.*
—James 5:7–8, ESV

Somehow autumn seems to be an American season: pumpkins, corn, candy
apples, Halloween, Vermont, and fall leaves. We experience this change in
temperature in our own private ways.

On the first cool afternoon this week, the first hint that summer was over,
I took a walk in the woods behind my parents' house, the same woods where
I used to play Robin Hood, bake apples with my brother, and hunt for sala-
manders under loose stones.

The fall aroma of the New Jersey woods is just as familiar to me now as it
was when I was a child: earthy, moist, a freshness to the air combined with a
slight chill that suggests the coming of winter. And I feel like a child again,
shrinking to a ten-year-old boy.

As I entered the woods, I thought about the Lenape Indians walking over
this same earth, passing the same rocks two hundred years ago. They were
sophisticated farmers of squash, corn, and kidney beans, and they hunted
birds, beavers, and deer.

I thought about how prevalent deer have become in New Jersey these past
fifty years. As a boy I never saw a deer, and today they roam our yards, appear
alongside our highways, and stare with startled looks when we stumble upon
them by accident, which is what happened in the woods the other day.

There were two: male and female. They were both young. The buck had one small horn protruding from the left side of his head. The doe was small and cautious.

I stood there and stared at the deer. They remained still and looked at me. Suddenly the buck stomped its right cloven hoof onto the ground. That startled me. I had never seen a deer do such a thing. I was insulted. It was being aggressive, and I was just standing there thinking of Bambi and Rudolf.

Usually when we come upon deer so suddenly, they turn and, like ballerinas, leap away with their white tales bouncing behind them. But not this pair. And then the buck did it again. He stomped his left hoof with the same thud and aggression. I thought for a second, *What will I do if he charges me?* I remembered those scenes in the Tarzan movies of people being trampled by elephants. As I took one step backward, both deer twisted around quickly and ran away into the distant brambles and disappeared.

When I turned away, I saw through the bushes and small trees what I thought was a large turtle. Something with a large, wide hump moved slowly in the dark shadows of the woods. I walked quietly (like a Lenape Indian!) toward the moving creature and suddenly recognized it as a huge turkey. The hump was the turkey's back and feathers as it lowered its head, pecking away for ants and grubs.

I walked as close to the turkey as I felt I could without being seen, and then I sat on the side of a fallen tree and watched. Then I realized that we were not alone; stepping out, as if from behind a magician's cloth, came six more full-grown turkeys. They, too, were pecking away at the ground, happily being turkeys. Little is more recognized as an American icon than a Thanksgiving turkey, and there I was in the woods among the ghosts of the American Indians with turkeys as big as the boy I once was.

After watching the flock for a few minutes, I quietly stepped backward and began to walk to the house when I came upon a spiderweb as big as a Frisbee, and in the center of the web a large, brown spider, E. B. White's Charlotte, perhaps.

E. B. White was an author in the American grain: a man of great intellect and humor, a prolific essay writer for *The New Yorker* magazine, and the famous writer of children's novels. He wrote in *Charlotte's Web*, "Children almost always hang onto things tighter than their parents think they will."

When I walked out of the woods, I grew back into a sixty-four-year-old man hanging on to my optimism and feeling that I had just stepped out of a Norman Rockwell painting.

Soon the maple and oak leaves will turn into the patchwork quilt of this new season, in this bold American autumn.

« »

God in Heaven, as you paint the fall season with your brush,
so paint continued colors of faith, hope, and charity
to my soul today.

33

Teacher

I will instruct you and teach you in the way you should go;
I will counsel you with my eye upon you.
—Psalm 32:8, ESV

I was a naive, lonely kid when I entered high school. I'd play a game when I stepped into the building each morning. I'd say to myself, "Let's see how many people will say hello to me in the hallway today." And 100 percent of the time the answer was zero, until I stepped into Mr. Emra's English class.

Bruce Emra was a new teacher. He laughed easily. I was impressed that he had a master's degree from New York University (and a beautiful Mercury Cougar), and he liked books, *The New Yorker* magazine, author John Updike, foreign movies, poetry, art, history, the Mets—and he seemed to like me.

I do not remember how the subject came up, but we were discussing in class the habits of the raccoon when I lamely said to Mr. Emra at the end of the period that I had pictures of raccoons that I had taken myself. He immediately asked if I would bring them in to show him. That night I rummaged through my disorganized desk drawer and pulled out my raccoon pictures.

I was delighted whenever I heard the metal garbage can lid fall to the ground outside the dining room window. I'd run to the window and see the tail and backside of a fat raccoon that had found, once again, something good for dinner deep inside the tall garbage can. I'd run to the basement window that was even with the garbage can, and there I'd watch the raccoon inches away.

One day I opened the basement window before the raccoon arrived to see if I could get a better look, and sure enough the raccoon didn't seem to care that I stood watching him as he happily knocked over the can and munched on cantaloupe rinds and stale bread. Then I had an idea. If I was so close to the raccoon, perhaps I could take pictures. That night I carried my Kodak Brownie camera and a flash attachment, and when the raccoon appeared, I snapped picture after picture. The raccoon passively looked at me, munched on his dinner, and, if I didn't know better, I'd say he smiled at me a few times in a pose of contentment and vanity.

When I brought these pictures to Mr. Emra, he looked at each one as if they were precious photographs from *National Geographic*. He laughed at the pictures, asked how I was able to get such close-up shots, and complimented me on my enthusiasm for these clever, agile creatures.

That year Mr. Emra had us sit in a circle as we discussed novels and short stories. We delighted in being in his class, where we got to know one another and learned to like one another as we worked on group projects. We spoke openly about ourselves and about our connections to the books we read. We wrote essays, plays, poems, and short stories, which meant that Mr. Emra spent countless hours at home reading our work and making personal comments on each of our papers: words of encouragement, suggestions for improvement, and kind praise.

It was in this class that Mr. Emra introduced me to the poetry of Dylan Thomas, particularly "Fern Hill" and read aloud Jean Shepherd's story "Wanda Hickey's Night of Golden Memories," and Updike's "A&P." In this class a teacher taught me that I was good, smart, charming, cheeky, and alive. I have carried that newly discovered confidence with me ever since.

Because of Mr. Emra's class, I walked through the high school halls with many people saying hello to me on a daily basis, and I have since walked through life with a sense of purpose, confidence, and joy about living, thanks to Mr. Emra and his interest in a goofy kid who liked raccoons.

"Hello!"

« »

Blessed are the teachers, for they have given us light.
Blessed are the teachers, for they have shown the way.

34

Fear

I sought the Lord, and he answered me;
he delivered me from all my fears.
—Psalm 34:4

Goblins, zombies, witches, and ghosts are the messengers of fright each Halloween, but we know that October thirty-first is not the only time we succumb to fear or create it intentionally.

When I was a boy, I noticed that my sister's new bed was perched on a high metal frame, leaving a great amount of space between the mattress and the floor. At the end of the evening, I rushed up to Anne's bedroom, crawled under her bed, and waited. I thought it would be a great joke to grab her ankles and scare her.

I heard my family climbing the stairs. I heard the door to my parents' bedroom close, and then I saw Anne's two feet. As she walked near the bed, I reached out, grabbed her ankles, and yelled, "YAHHHHH!"

I laughed as she crumpled to the floor. I expected that she, too, would laugh. Instead she gave out a chilling cry of distress and fear and began sobbing. My father rushed into the room as I quickly scooted back under the bed. When my dad leaned over and looked at me in the semidarkness, I knew that I was the devil, condemned to my bedroom for days with the promise that I would never frighten my sister again.

But I, too, was a victim. Why is it that brothers like to dare each other? "I dare you to eat a mustard sandwich," or "I dare you to jump off the garage roof." My brother said one night with a snicker, "I dare you to run behind the chicken coop and tear a bit off the red chair and bring it back."

The red chair was a portly piece of stuffed furniture made of coarse material. When it finally split open from wear, my father dumped it behind the chicken coop, on the dark side of the yard. It was the place that bordered the woods, where snakes and brambles shared the terrain, and where I had always imagined that the bones of the cats we had buried there would rise up and chase me to my own death.

"Chrissie," my brother repeated, "I dare you to run to the back of the chicken coop, rip off a piece of the chair, and bring it back as proof that you are not an old baby."

I refused, but in the safe morning light I did walk to the forbidden part of the property, rip a small piece off the red chair, and tuck it into my pocket. I kept it with me until the next night when my brother made the same dark dare, calling me a "double baby." I stood up in the living room with bravado, walked out of the house, stood on the back porch for a moment, and when I returned with the evidence of my bravery, I was the hero for the night. Boys are easily frightened, but clever, too.

But I was not so clever about the man in the pine tree. I was coming home late from school one October day. It was dusk. The clouds were dark. The trees began to look like giant monsters leaning down over me as I walked down the driveway. The rhododendron bush began to look like a giant wart. There was a noise in the pine tree to my right. I looked up and nearly fell backward with fright. Two eyes looked down at me in a menacing manner—two probing eyes that I knew must belong to a man hiding in the tree, ready to jump and kill me.

Suddenly there was a huge rustling. The "man" spread his wings like a devil. I screamed until I realized that this ghost, this goblin, was a large owl. I heard its wings whoosh in the air as it flew up and disappeared over the house.

I am many years past that night, but this is the season when Dracula rings my doorbell, when Frankenstein digs his hand into a bowl of candy corn and chocolate.

"Double, double toil and trouble; fire burn and caldron bubble," said the witches in William Shakespeare's *Macbeth*.

May your troubles and fears be soothed in the Halloween caldron; may you watch out for owls and brothers. And, if you need it, I have an extra piece of that red chair.

Boo!

« »

Praise the Lord for he speaks comfort with his voice.
Praise the Lord for his reassuring hands that reach out to us.
May the Lord protect us and vanquish our fears.

35

Magical Pumpkins

Enter his gates with thanksgiving, and his courts with praise!
Give thanks to him; bless his name!
—Psalm 100:4, ESV

Charles Schulz, the creator of the *Peanuts* cartoon strip, wrote a little story about a boy who believes there is such a thing as the Great Pumpkin. Linus believes in himself and in the existence of the mythical being to the degree that he gives up trick-or-treating and stays up until four in the morning, waiting and watching for the appearance of this magical pumpkin that will rise from the most deserving pumpkin patch and distribute gifts to children all over the world.

Of course, there is no magical pumpkin in Linus's pumpkin patch, but no matter; I still believe in the magic and delight of the pumpkin in this autumn month of October.

The first important pumpkin in my life was the one my sister Anne and I rescued from the farm behind our house. Pumpkins are good feed for cattle, and our neighbor, who owned the last farm in our little town, raised pumpkins and tossed them into his field where he kept a single dairy cow. Most of the pumpkins broke open as they were heaved over the fence, but Anne and I saw from the safety of our woods a large, orange pumpkin that was whole and sitting helplessly beside the hungry-looking cow. Because the farmer was nowhere in sight, we scrambled under the barbed wire fence, raced to the pumpkin (I saluted the cow), and then rolled the pumpkin back into our woods.

It was the biggest pumpkin I'd ever had, along with the biggest guilt I felt as a child for stealing the pumpkin from our neighbor. But I must admit, it did look good sitting on the front steps of our house so many years ago.

Consider the following magical pumpkin delights:

- Massaging ground pumpkin paste onto the face was once believed to be a method for removing freckles.
- The word *pumpkin* derives from the Greek word *pepon,* meaning "large melon."
- Morton, Illinois, has earned the title of the Pumpkin Capital of the World, as 85 percent of the world's canned pumpkin is produced there.
- Cinderella's fairy godmother turned a pumpkin into a beautiful carriage.
- Pumpkin juice is the favorite drink of the students at the Hogwarts School in the Harry Potter novels.
- The famous American writer Henry David Thoreau said, "I would rather sit on a pumpkin and have it all to myself, than be crowded on a velvet cushion."
- Peter, Peter, pumpkin-eater kept his wife in a pumpkin shell.
- In his poem "The Pumpkin," the poet and abolitionist John Greenleaf Whittier wrote, "What moistens the lip and what brightens the eye? What calls back the past, like the rich Pumpkin pie?"

When my two sons and one daughter were children, they loved sitting at the kitchen table with me and their mother as we all carved four pumpkins for Halloween. They each had a small pumpkin, and I was in charge of the big one, until it was time to pull out all the goo and seeds, which the children liked to do with their bare hands.

The children liked to recite this nursery rhyme:

Five little pumpkins sitting on a gate.
The first one said, "Oh my it's getting late."
The second one said, "There are witches in the air."
The third one said, "But we don't care!"
The fourth one said, "Let's run and run and run."

The fifth one said, "I'm ready for some fun!"
"Woooooo" went the wind,
And out went the lights.
And the five little pumpkins rolled out of sight.

I remember how much the children liked to repeat the line "'Woooooo' went the wind, and out went the lights" and how much I enjoyed telling the children that it was time for bed, time for three little pumpkins to roll out of sight.

For the past thirty-seven years, I have placed a large plastic pumpkin with a light in its belly in my window, here in this little room where I write. This is the best place to see it from the street at night—a lighted pumpkin with its crooked teeth and broad smile, and with its upside-down pyramid eyes and pyramid pumpkin nose.

By November 1, all the nation's pumpkins will fall from the gate and roll out of sight as we march toward Christmas.

I miss my children and their gooey hands in the kitchen.

Let's moisten our lips. Let's sit in the pumpkin patch with Linus (not on a velvet chair). Let's sit with the boy and with his unbending faith that the Great Pumpkin will appear and bless us this year.

Pumpkins may be 90 percent water, but I think the other 10 percent is magic—and it is the magic that makes all the difference in the world.

« »

We are amazed with the magic of your love, O Lord.

36

Illumination

*Now I have heard about you that a spirit of the gods is in you,
and that illumination, insight and extraordinary wisdom
have been found in you.*
—Daniel 5:14, NASB

All I wanted to do was to light my pumpkin for the children who would soon be ringing my doorbell dressed as pirates, witches, princesses, and ghosts.

Each year I climb the rickety pull-down attic stairs, crawl under the rafters of the house, and grab the tall, stout plastic pumpkin hidden in the dark behind the Christmas boxes and suitcases.

I realize a plastic pumpkin is not as charming and old-world as a real pumpkin, and I do miss out on the fun of cutting the pumpkin open, reaching inside, and pulling out all the pulp, goo, and seeds. Carving pumpkins is, in many ways, an event reserved for children to do with their fathers or mothers, but my children are all adults. They left behind a dollhouse, a train set, a rock collection, and their old father in the attic, so while I do not carve pumpkins any longer for Halloween, I still like to carry down my plastic pumpkin I bought long after the children left home, and prop it up at the front window, even if it is fake with an electric bulb in its belly.

That was the problem. When I set up the pumpkin on a small table so that it faced the outside, framed in the window, I plugged in the light. Nothing. No light. The inside of the pumpkin was as dark as the attic, perhaps how *my* insides feel when I think about my missing children.

I climbed back up into the attic and found a box of Christmas lights, just the right size for the pumpkin's light. I grabbed one, climbed down the stairs for the second time, returned to my weak pumpkin, unscrewed the bulb, and replaced it with the new one. Nothing. The pumpkin's eyes, nose, and mouth remained dark holes that seemed to stare at me with contempt.

It must be the fuse, I thought. I grabbed the end of the electric cord where the fuse was encased in a small plastic box. I slid back the small protective cover, stared at the fuse, and said to myself, looks good to me. I grabbed a pen, thinking all it needed was a bit of wiggling, but then I stupidly punctured the fuse with the pen point and small bits of glass scattered onto the floor. Well at least I knew for sure that the fuse was now broken. So, I drove to the hardware store.

One of the most famous hardware stores in Morris County is Jones Hardware on the Newark Pompton Turnpike in Pompton Plains, famous because Robbie Jones inherited his father's know-how and kindness along with the store itself.

Ask for an obscure bolt, and Robbie will have it. Ask for an old-fashioned doorbell, and Robbie will reach over and magically produce it. Robbie will even give you advice on how to raise children or chickens or how to caulk a bathtub, or what paint to buy. So I knew, I just knew, that Jones Hardware would have a tiny half-inch fuse for the heart of my pumpkin.

I unscrewed the bottom of the pumpkin, drove to the store, and walked in with the cord, that empty fuse container, and my frustration.

"Five AMP fuse?" Robbie asked right away as if he was expecting me. I had no idea what AMP I needed (I admit I still don't even know what an AMP is), but I nodded dumbly. "It's for my pumpkin."

Within seconds, Robbie was squeezing the new fuse into the cord's container, and then he plugged in the light. Nothing.

"It's the bulb," I said with authority. "I must have knocked it against the chair when I tried to adjust the pumpkin."

Robbie looked at the bulb, and then he looked at me. "Seems fine to me. The filament is still intact."

"No, no, that's okay. It's the bulb. I have many at home."

After I paid for the fuse, I drove home feeling strong, confident, and triumphant. I live in a man's world, and I had just accomplished a man's task at the hardware store.

Of course, when I replaced the bulb with *another* bulb from the attic, the light still didn't work. If it's not the bulb, if it's not the fuse, it must be me! I looked at the pumpkin. It just kept mocking me with its silly, toothless grin.

"Yeah?" I said to the pumpkin, "I know a headless horseman who'd be happy to have you propped up on his shoulders as he rides through Washington Irving's Sleepy Hollow." The pumpkin just continued to smirk.

Finally, I had an idea. I climbed back up into the attic for the third time, grabbed one of the Christmas candles we place in the windows each winter, stuck the candle inside the pumpkin, and plugged it in, and suddenly the pumpkin glowed with soft orange light emanating from its eyes, nose, and mouth.

It is Halloween again. The candy is ready. Children are wiggling into their costumes once again, and my pumpkin is illuminated in the window—my old, stout pumpkin, like me, grinning that he still has a few good years left in him after all.

« »

Lord I pray that you keep your light illuminated
deep within my soul so that I may continue
to share the good news.

37

Soldier

Flowers appear on the earth;
The seasons of singing has come
The cooing of doves
Is heard in our land.
—Song of Solomon 2:12

In July of 1914, during World War I, my grandfather, a career soldier in the Belgian army, was so severely wounded in his left arm that the surgeons couldn't determine if they should cut his arm off at the shoulder or the elbow. He begged the doctors not to cut off his arm, and when he woke up from the operation, he slowly patted his left side: shoulder, elbow . . . hand. His arm was saved, but because there was no such thing as microsurgery at the time, it was a useless appendage hanging from his left side for the rest of his life. If that bullet had entered my grandfather's body just twelve more inches to the right, I would not have been born.

During World War II, my grandfather once again faced an invading army, composed, this time, of Hitler's Nazi troops in May of 1940. My grandfather quickly joined the Belgian underground, a resistance movement called La Dame Blanche, created during World War I, that provided information and troop movements to the allies and caused as much havoc for the German troops as possible.

By luck, my grandfather heard that the elite SS Nazis had gotten wind of his activities, and he fled Belgium and escaped to Spain, where he was captured and placed in a prison camp. But then he became part of an exchange program between England and Spain in which England traded gasoline for English prisoners of war.

During his four years in England, my grandfather broadcast encouraging words to his country and helped thousands of European refugees who were able to escape to England, and at the end of the war he was a significant player in the reconstruction of Europe, receiving personal awards from General Dwight Eisenhower and British General Bernard Montgomery.

My grandfather also loved flowers. When he retired from the army as a full general, he came to America every two years with my grandmother. I was only a boy, afraid of his stern look and charmed by his gentle smile. Boys like war stories: tanks exploding, torpedoes sinking ships, but my grandfather never spoke about the wars. I watched him plant lilies, pansies, purple irises, and roses—beautiful white roses. During the summer, he spent much of his time weeding, creating garden borders, and loosening the earth with a small trowel. I would watch him as he knelt on one knee, propping his damaged arm onto his knee as he leaned over and worked the soil with his good right hand.

I spent a recent weekend with my mother in the house where I grew up. She is ninety-four years old: vibrant and optimistic. She continues to read *The New Yorker* magazine, travel books, and novels. She continues to write. Her political opinions are sharp and completely immersed in up-to-date points of view. As she was preparing dinner, she asked that I go see if I could find any late summer flowers left in the garden for the dining room table.

I grabbed a small pair of pruning shears and stepped out into the yard. There is not much of a garden left. The apple tree fell in the early 1970s. The raspberry bushes withered away many years ago. The current year's daylilies had succumbed to the cold September air. There were no more irises, but there, clinging to what was left of the rosebush, was one white rose.

I thought of the white gloves that I had seen on my grandfather's hands in many pictures of him in his general's uniform. I thought of his smile and what he did to help preserve freedom for everyone in the world.

I looked at that single flower: white petals overlapping like folds in the ocean tide, the stem with its strong grip on the flower. I thought how my grandfather planted that rosebush more than sixty years ago. I secretly thanked my grandfather for the roses and for my life.

I didn't cut off the flower. Grateful for its existence, I let it hang there at the side of the bush, preserving the last bit of beauty in the garden for all seasons, preserving the memory of what a single flower can do for the world that struggles each day for a bit of peace.

« »

Blessed are the peacemakers.

38

The End of Something

For this is the message you heard from the beginning: We should love one another. Do not be like Cain, who belonged to the evil one and murdered his brother. And why did he murder him? Because his own actions were evil and his brother's were righteous.
—1 John 3:11–12

On November 22, 1963, President John F. Kennedy was assassinated at Dealey Plaza in Dallas, Texas, at 1:30 p.m. Eastern Standard Time. I was twelve years old and share with all who remember that tragic moment. Like everyone else, I remember exactly where I was: in Mr. Odo's seventh-grade class taking a dreaded spelling quiz.

While I was trying unsuccessfully to pass the quiz, the principal quietly entered the room that early afternoon, walked up to Mr. Odo, leaned over, and whispered in his left ear, just loud enough for me to hear: "The president has been shot."

In 1963, I didn't know that George C. Wallace became governor of Alabama and proclaimed loudly, "Segregation now, segregation tomorrow, and segregation forever!" I caught fireflies in the backyard with a mayonnaise jar.

I didn't know that the poet Sylvia Plath committed suicide in England. In 1963, I saw the movie *Lawrence of Arabia*.

I didn't know in 1963 that Medgar Evers was murdered in Jackson, Mississippi. I had my first crush on a girl: Loretta.

I didn't even know that on August 28, 1963, Martin Luther King Jr. delivered his "I Have a Dream" speech. I watched *The Flintstones* on television and *My Three Sons*, and *The Wonderful World of Disney*. (Yes, I owned a Davy Crockett coonskin hat.)

In the movie *Lawrence of Arabia*, a club secretary says to Lawrence, "I say, Lawrence. You are a clown!" To which he answers, "Ah, well, we can't all be lion tamers."

In 1963, I wasn't a clown; I was just a boy. I was naive to the world's events and more interested in Loretta's giggles than I was in anything that Walter Cronkite had to say. But then on Friday, November 22, 1963, I walked home from school and saw my father cry for the first time, and I watched as Mr. Cronkite slipped off his glasses on national television and announced to the world that President Kennedy had died.

On Monday, November 25, I watched the funeral procession with the rest of the nation as President Kennedy's coffin was carried through the streets of Washington, D.C., on a caisson drawn by beautiful white horses. I watched a little boy salute his father's flag-draped casket. That was the weekend my childhood came to an end.

Many years later, President Kennedy's sister, Eunice Kennedy Shriver, invited me to her home outside Washington, D.C., to help her write a speech she was to give at the fortieth anniversary of the Joseph P. Kennedy Foundation.

Before we sat at her kitchen table to draft the speech together, she walked me into the living room and to a large piece of furniture. On the flat, polished surface were many, many photographs of the entire Kennedy family: John, Bobby, Ted, Joseph, Eunice, Rosemary, Kathleen, Patricia, Jean. There was Sargent Shriver with his children, and Eunice with her parents. They all looked young and happy and at ease in their sweaters and sneakers and on their sailboats and on their lawns playing touch football.

I said to Mrs. Kennedy, "I am so sorry for the suffering your family endured." She looked at the wide collection of pictures, and with a broad sweep of her confident hand she said, "Faith and prayer."

At a special message to Congress in 1962, President Kennedy said:

Our deep spiritual confidence that this nation will survive the perils of today—which may well be with us for decades to come—compels us to invest in our nation's future, to consider and meet our obligations to our children and the numberless generations that will follow.

"Faith and prayer" Eunice Kennedy said. "Spiritual confidence," her brother reminded us.

They say that the baby boomer generation created for our nation a time of both rejection and redemption. Many of us, like the Kennedy family, chose redemption and still struggle with faith and prayer.

May all of us baby boomers wrap ourselves in a Woodstock blanket, sing some Beatle songs together, and instruct our children and grandchildren to ask not what their country can do for them, but ask them what they can do for their country.

Let us live in celebration of gratitude, stillness, and laughter. Let us baby boomers teach the numberless generations that will follow us to trust in faith and prayer and to be lion tamers.

« »

God, help me that I too may be a lion tamer.

WINTER

Song falls silent, music is dumb,
But the air burns with their fragrance,
And white winter, on its knees,
Observes everything with reverent attention.

—Anna Akhmatova

39

Rosebud

Then Jacob kissed Rachel, and lifted his voice and wept.
—Genesis 29:11, NKJV

There was a time when snow was the most important part of my life. Boys don't often tell about their secrets. Mine was a fascination with snow. If there was a forecast on the radio calling for snow in the evening, I'd lie on my bed and place my chin on the windowsill and wait. The back-porch light was always lit at night, and if there was the slightest chance of snow, I'd see the first white flakes swirling in the yard like little bits of paper.

But it wasn't just the snow that held my attention. It was the coming adventure: the sledding. I wasn't good at football, baseball, or basketball. I wasn't good at any sport, but I knew how to maneuver a sled down the long hill on our neighbor's property. There, in the moonlight or the full afternoon sun, I was the champion.

There is something in a child's DNA that makes him feel bold and brave as he drags his sled uphill behind him with a small rope as his black boots with the metal clips clop, clop in the snow.

Walking up that hill with my sisters and brother and with Johnny and Patty next door was like winding up a toy race car with a magic key. When I stood at the top of the hill, I was ready—the spring in my boy-heart was ready to be released, and then I'd run with the sled in my hands. "Gangway!" I'd shout. *The Olympic sled boy is at the starting gate!* I'd imagine as I dropped the sled onto the snow and jump on, belly down, arms extended to the handles. Down, down, down, the sleigh boy, wonder boy, magic boy zoomed on the white snow, the fast snow.

The sled wasn't mine. It was large and red and belonged to my brother. My parents bought it at the Junior Exchange, the used clothing store that also sold secondhand appliances, toys, roller skates, and sleds. Most of my clothes were bought at the Junior Exchange, as were my skates, my bike, and the red sled. My parents couldn't afford much, but they knew how to keep me warm and how to feed my adventures.

Before we had the sled, we'd use cardboard boxes, or, as they did in the movie *It's a Wonderful Life*, we'd use shovels.

As I grew older, I lost interest in sledding, but I must admit that when I saw Dr. Zhivago and Lara in the old version of the movie, I felt a tug. There they were on their way in the snow, being pulled by the horse, the bells jingling, the snow blowing in their faces. They were happy together. That is how I felt when I went sledding as a boy: just happy.

We never know what specific moment will become an iconic memory that will stay with us and sustain us when we are old and in need of solace.

In high school I had the nerve to ask Sue Anderson, one of the prettiest girls in the school, if she wanted to get together Saturday night. It was winter, and, to my astonishment, she said yes. I suggested we go sledding over on Sam's Hill, which is now filled with large homes and swimming pools.

I walked into the garage and found behind old window screens and dust the red sled I hadn't used in over ten years. I ran a bar of soap on the iron runners and moved the handles back and forth to see if they still worked. They did.

That night, Sue and I zoomed down Sam's Hill, she clutching my waist as I'd seen the girls do on the backs of motorcycles. She was cold. It began to rain. We decided to leave. That was our only time together. I should have kissed her.

In the film *Citizen Kane*, Charles Foster Kane, the wealthy newspaper mogul, clawed his way through life by stepping on everyone to gain power, and at the end of his selfish existence, he uttered a final word: "Rosebud." It was the name of the sled from his childhood, and it was on that sled that he had felt the happiest.

I've lived a long life according to the actuarial studies. I married well. Roe and I have three grown children, all making a difference in the world. My cat Stuart sits on my lap as I write these words.

Grown men understand the complications of happiness; a boy, well, he just zooms down a hill of fresh snow with a girl clinging to his waist, or he shouts to his sisters and brothers, "Gangway!"

I don't know what happened to the big red sled. I looked for it in my mother's garage, in her basement, and in my cluttered memory somewhere back, back when the radio announced that it would snow tomorrow and I would place my chin on the cold windowsill and wait.

Give me a sled and a girl and winter, and I am seventeen all over again.

« »

Thank you, Lord, for those precious memories,
for they sustain me when I am alone.

40

Snow

He spreads the snow like wool
and scatters the frost like ashes.
—Psalm 147:16

Do you remember Maurice Sendak's charming monsters in his keenly illustrated children's book *Where the Wild Things Are*? I think of these dreamlike
creatures whenever I hear the announcement of an impending snowstorm
heading our way.

The way the media hypes the coming onslaught, the way we rush to the
supermarkets to stock up on food, makes me imagine the abominable snow-
man stomping down from the north, an eighth "wild thing" in thick white
fur, swinging from the winter branches with Max, the boy sent to his room for
misbehaving.

While I recognize that snow is a hazard and that television executives want
to stir up the public's attention and fear so they can sell commercial space, I'd
like to consider, too, that snow is also a community reminder of what is gentle
and, in some ways, purifying.

I'd rather have the words of Ralph Waldo Emerson at the top of the news
hour in the middle of winter: "Announced by all the trumpets of the sky,
arrives the snow." I am now in my sixties, and I can still say with certitude that
I look to the gray sky with a boy's delight whenever there is a prediction of
snow. Announcing the coming of snow with trumpets still seems right to me.
Snow means sledding, and snowball fights, and snowmen, and snow angels.
Snow means snow caves and tracking rabbits. I am glad that I grew up in the
fifties and sixties. I was not distracted from outdoor pleasures by video games
and cell phones.

Back then, I spent many hours following rabbit tracks in the woods, hoping to find where the rabbits lived, sure that the tracks would lead me to some magical place where rabbits wore slippers and drank carrot soup from wooden bowls.

We take for granted that snow is inevitable in much of our country, but few people recognize the nearly monastic opportunity snow offers us with each new storm. A monastery is a place of solitude and quiet, a place for contemplation in the silence. Have you ever walked in the woods after a heavy snowfall? Have you ever walked through an open meadow covered with fresh snow? What did you notice? Yes, the silence. Fresh snow acts as a sound-absorbing material, much like what a new carpet does for an empty room. Air between the accumulated snowflakes traps the sound and minimizes the vibrations—hence, a muted, holy silence. Joseph Conrad had the title right in his short story about a quiet little boy: "Silent Snow, Secret Snow."

As a child I always felt a certain affinity with the silence in winter, as though the snow was something all-embracing, protecting the secret of me.

Ezra Jack Keats, the children's book author and illustrator, created one of his most renowned books, *The Snowy Day*. It is a simple story about a city boy, Peter, who wakes up in his apartment and, with delight, sees that it has snowed during the night. The boy bundles up, walks along the sidewalk, drags his feet in the snow, finds a wonderful stick, makes a line in the snow, watches boys in a snowball fight, climbs mountains of snow. He even tries to save a snowball in his pocket.

One of my happiest moments in college was grabbing two plastic trays from the dining hall and sliding down the hill along the main campus with Kathy the biology major beside me as she laughed and laughed all the way down to the bottom, where I planned to kiss her.

I'll admit that snow can be formidable. During the 1998–1999 season, Mt. Baker outside of Bellingham, Washington, recorded the world record for total snowfall: 1,140 inches! Frightful avalanches have crushed people and whole villages. Highways are clogged, planes delayed and canceled.

But snowflakes on the tongue are like pretend candy. A part of us is left behind on the wings of the snow angels. The poet Wallace Stevens had it right in his poem "The Snow Man": "One must have a mind of winter / To regard the frost and the boughs / Of the pine-trees crusted with snow."

I have kept the mind of winter in my own way, grappling with my monsters of waning youth and ill health. But when I hear trumpets and the snow comes, I call to mind my own wild things: Peter and Max and the biology major from college. I hand out the plastic trays, and we all zoom down the hill along the white, pure snow, something far better than the Yellow Brick Road, a path back to happier times, a moment in winter when all does seem silent, secret, and safe.

« »

Let us pray for hints of God:
Snow, like his love, covers the world.

41

Christmas

For this child I prayed . . .
—1 Samuel 1:27, ESV

When I finally finished raking leaves in the yard a few weeks ago, I walked back across the lawn like a happy Snow White dwarf, knowing that my work in the autumn garden was complete for another season. Feeling accomplished and still filled with energy, I decided, before putting the rake away, to clean the shed, rearrange the tools and flowerpots, and toss out old bags of fertilizer and broken chairs.

I pulled out the wheelbarrow, the lawnmower, a tangled badminton net, an old tent, a shovel, a pick, a wagon, and then I noticed, sitting on the shelf to the right and in the dark, the castle. I hadn't noticed the castle in years.

When Roe and I moved into our small house in Pompton Plains, New Jersey, forty years ago, we carried in our tiny U-Haul trailer my college refrigerator, our clothes, a bed, and my castle. It is made from plywood and is the size of a small microwave oven. The walls are yellow; the moat is green. It has a drawbridge that works, and neatly cut jagged wall toppers, or battlements, that define my castle as something medieval and magical.

But the best thing about my castle? My father made it for me one Christmas many years ago when I was a boy and he was a young man.

Sometimes I thought of my father as Geppetto, the clever toymaker who could create a boy from wood. While working as a college professor, writer, and editor, my father sometimes made wooden swords for us children, airplanes that flew, weaving looms that worked, a bed for my sister's dolls . . . and a castle for me.

One year my father built for my brother Bruno a gray castle with a high turret. He even painted a coat of arms on the outside wall, so there was no question in my mind when I was asked what I'd like for Christmas that year. "A castle, like Bruno's! That's what I'd like for Christmas!"

Beginning in November 1962, when my father descended into the basement, I was gently told that I was not to join him. Even though I was pretty sure that he was working on my Christmas gift, children have a cruel imagination that sometimes taunts them. "Maybe he's not making a castle. Maybe he's making another silly bed for my sister's dolls."

When I asked my mother if Daddy was building a castle in the basement, she'd smile, pretend she didn't know what I was talking about, and then send me off to do my homework.

During the following weeks, I slipped down into the basement when no one was around and never found anything that even resembled a castle.

In the middle of December, I had to know. After dinner one evening, my father stood up from the kitchen table and said that he would be spending some time in the basement. I volunteered to join him, but my mother said that I was to leave my father alone. So my brothers and sisters and I rushed into the living room and probably watched *The Flintstones*, *McHale's Navy*, or *My Three Sons*. I was lying on the floor watching television when I heard a small, rhythmic tapping sound beneath me. I just had to know what my father was doing.

I stood up, pretending that I had to go to the bathroom, and ran out of the living room, took a left, ran to the hall closet, yanked out my winter coat, and sneaked out the front door. I made a right, ran down the driveway of crunchy stones toward the garage, opened the green garden gate, ran across the lawn, jumped down the rock stairs, made another right, and slowly crept to the basement window that glowed in the dark like a slab of thin honeycomb.

I could hear from inside the basement that tapping, tapping, tapping. I felt that I had to crawl up to the window like a spy, and when I looked inside the basement, there, under the dim light bulb, was my father in his white shirt with his sleeves rolled up. He was wearing his horn-rimmed glasses and leaning over his workbench, nailing together those wonderful castle walls.

At the time, I didn't know that, as I watched my father, I was really looking at Santa Claus.

I received a fine yellow castle that Christmas morning, and I was happy, and it was the centerpiece of many battles with my plastic soldiers and marbles over the years, and then I discovered the Beatles and girls and high school and college and marriage and then carried an old wooden castle to the garden shed of my new home, where it was forgotten. The season changed. The babies were born. The years passed. My father died.

I didn't realize at the time that one of the best parts of that Christmas was the anticipation of receiving the castle. And now it has become the postcard in my memory of a small boy looking at his father among the tools and fresh sawdust, watching the man who helped turn a little wooden boy into a sixty-seven-year-old man who still delights in the ownership of a yellow castle with a working drawbridge.

Merry Christmas, Dad.

《 》

When I am tired, I hear the cry of the Christ child.
When I am alone, I see the star of Bethlehem.
When I feel defeated, I follow the path of the three kings.
Grant me strength, community, victory, Child of God,
Child of light. Noel. Noel. Noel.

42

The True Light of Christmas

The way of the wicked is like darkness;
they do not know over what they stumble.
—Proverbs 4:19, NASB

If you go to the Morgan Library & Museum in New York City, you can see, in Charles Dickens's own handwriting, the original manuscript of *A Christmas Carol*. You can see the words of Ebenezer Scrooge before the miserable businessman had his epiphany: "Every idiot who goes about with 'Merry Christmas' on his lips, should be boiled with his own pudding, and buried with a stake of holly through his heart."

If you turn on the television this Christmas season, you are likely to see Frank Capra's iconic film *It's a Wonderful Life*, where the greedy, crude banker Mr. Potter says, "George, I am an old man and most people hate me. But I don't like them, either, so that makes it all even. You know just as well as I do that I run practically everything in this town but the Bailey Building and Loan. You know, also, that for a number of years, I've been trying to get control of it. Or kill it."

If you turn to the Gospels, you will read that over 2,000 years ago King Herod, with his ego and envy, heard that a new king was born in a small village called Bethlehem, so he ordered the slaying of all baby boys in the region because he feared his authority would be threatened by a more powerful monarch.

Do we live in a new world where our leaders govern because of their insecurities and hunger for power? Do we live in Pottersville, where money and strength take precedence over humility and compassion? Do we live in a country where poverty, hunger, medical needs, and sorrow are greeted with a single phrase: "Bah, humbug"?

Recently, for the thirty-ninth time, my wife and I drove to the Christmas tree farm we visit each December. I brought a small saw; she brought mittens and hot chocolate.

The past few years, I'd kept my disappointment to myself: same tree farm, same walk among the trees, same "This one is too short; this one is too thin." I miss the days when our three children ran ahead of us. "This one, Daddy! This one!"

In *The Unbearable Lightness of Being*, the novelist Milan Kundera wrote: "Everything is illuminated by the aura of nostalgia." I miss the way my daughter's face lit up when we began to decorate the tree in the living room. I miss walking with my father down to the Methodist church to visit the life-sized nativity that was lit up with a soft spotlight.

Each year in our little town of Pompton Plains, Robbie Jones sets up Santa and his reindeer on top of his hardware store, and each year I look for the small, red-lit nose of Rudolf. Again, I place a single electric candle in each of our windows. I try to keep the true light of Christmas burning.

But the world's lights seem to be dimming. I admit that I find myself more and more crying out for nostalgia, wishing things didn't change.

In *The Old Man and the Sea*, Ernest Hemingway wrote that the old man "no longer dreamed of storms, nor of women, nor of great occurrences, nor of great fish, nor fights, nor contests of strength, nor of his wife. He only dreamed of places now and the lions on the beach."

It is hard these days to dream of great occurrences and great fish and contests of strength and goodness and compassion and holiness and Christmas and God and joy when Herod is still trying to kill the baby in Bethlehem, when Pottersville is spreading throughout the country, when the Scrooge side of our national psyche is weaving into our lives with threads of ego, greed, and fear.

« »

Lord, protect us from evil, equip us with the light of your love.
Guide us through the darkness, and place our hands on your face,
so that we recognize you even with our eyes closed.

43

The Meaning of Christmas

And there were in the same country shepherds abiding in the field.
—Luke 2:8–14, KJV

Each year in our town the lampposts are decorated with wreaths and lights. Driving through our little town between the barbershop and the dry cleaner's, I feel like shouting out my window, "Merry Christmas, Bedford Falls!" half expecting George Bailey to call back, "and a Merry Christmas to you, Chris!"

When I was a boy, one of the local churches in my hometown of Allendale recreated a life-sized nativity during each Christmas season. The tall statues of the shepherds wore fur vests; the crib was filled with real straw. I remember standing in awe with my parents as we visited this particular nativity scene. There were spotlights illuminating Mary's face. A sheep sat beside the crib. The baby seemed warm and comfortable. Behind me, my parents stood in the darkness and cold as my mother whispered, "See, Christopher?"

Do we have to fight our way back to celebrating the true meaning of Christmas?

In David Michaelis's splendid book *Schulz and Peanuts: A Biography*, he chronicles how the famous creator of Charlie Brown and *A Charlie Brown Christmas* "insisted that the season's true meaning could be found in the Gospel according to St. Luke, and they agreed that the show would somehow work in the nativity story." However, the producer was concerned, especially when Mr. Schulz, according to Michaelis's biography, announced proudly that "one whole minute" of Linus reciting the Gospel would be part of the animated story.

The television world, the producer, and the sponsors were uncomfortable with this portion of the project, but then Charles Schulz insisted, "We can't avoid it. We have to get the passage of St. Luke in there somehow. If we don't do it, who will?"

And so, in 1965, after Charlie Brown asked if anyone knew what Christmas was all about, Linus van Pelt, on broadcast television, stood before the Peanuts gang on the rehearsal stage and recited these words:

> And there were in the same country shepherds abiding in the field, keeping watch over their flock by night. And, lo, the angel of the Lord came upon them, and the glory of the Lord shone round about them: and they were sore afraid. And the angel said unto them, Fear not: for, behold, I bring you good tidings of great joy, which shall be to all people. For unto you is born this day in the city of David a Savior, which is Christ the Lord. And this shall be a sign unto you; Ye shall find the babe wrapped in swaddling clothes, lying in a manger. And suddenly there was with the angel a multitude of the heavenly host praising God, and saying, Glory to God in the highest, and on earth peace, good will toward men.

From century to century the message has been handed down to us, and today we recognize, still, hints of hope in the whisper of a mother saying, "See?" and in the little cartoon of a boy saying, "On earth peace, good will toward men."

Despite all the world's sorrows, in the face of our national and personal tragedies, we still recognize, deep within ourselves, that it is a wonderful life.

For many people, Christmas is a historical reality, and for others a religious reality, but no matter how we look upon this event, as the Grinch thought in Dr. Seuss's book, "Maybe Christmas . . . doesn't come from a store."

« »

Lord, remind me that the true gift was wrapped
in swaddling clothes in Bethlehem under the star of hope.

44

O Holy Night

When the angels had gone away from them into heaven,
the shepherds began saying to one another,
"Let us go straight to Bethlehem then, and see this thing
that has happened which the Lord has made known to us."
—Luke 2:15, NASB

Although the historical facts have been debated concerning the child who was probably born in Bethlehem, we recognize today that something extraordinary happened a little over 2,000 years ago that has stitched itself into all that we read, all that we believe, and all that we do in our daily lives regardless of what religion we live, what language we speak, or what customs we've inherited. Somehow many of us feel a certain something during the Christmas season that manages to cut through the commercial hype that seems to blur the central reality of December 25.

As it happens in so many high schools across the United States, there is, always, the nostalgic Christmas concert here in our small township of Pequannock. "O Holy Night," the famous Christmas carol created by the French composer Adolphe Adam in 1847 was, in 1906, the first song ever broadcast on the radio. This was also the last song the Pequannock High School students sang year after year in their Christmas concerts conducted by William Cromie, a good man who died on May 5 at the age of seventy-three.

Each year, Mr. Cromie, a forty-year veteran teacher and choir director, invited the alumni choir members to join him and the students for the annual singing of this song.

After Mr. Cromie arranged the returning adults on the stage and made quiet jokes with his students past and present, he'd face his choir, raise his hands, command attention, and then, with a slight movement, all of Christmas seemed to flow from the lungs and souls of Mr. Cromie's choir.

For years and years, after the very last words of the song: "His power and glory ever more proclaim!" Mr. Cromie spun around, faced the audience, and with robust fervor called out, "Merry Christmas!"

For many people in our community, Christmas didn't begin until Mr. Cromie's celebrated conclusion to the holiday concert. He was a man who believed in Charles Dickens's words: "I will honor Christmas in my heart, and try to keep it all the year."

« »

Noel in our hearts each day,
Noel in our hearts each month,
Noel in our hearts year-round,
Noel! Noel! Noel!

45

Who Are We?

So God created man in his own image,
in the image of God he created them;
male and female he created them.
—Genesis 1:27

I once thought that I might be Santa Claus. It was a feeling that a werewolf probably has, the notion that deep inside there is something other than the visible self.

When the actress Maureen O'Hara died, a part of my baby boomer self also died. She was best known for her role as Doris Walker, the director of events at the Macy's department store in New York City in the movie *Miracle on 34th Street*. Poor Doris was harried, cynical, and didn't believe that Kris Kringle was really Santa Claus.

When I heard that Miss O'Hara had died, I felt an urge to go to the Macy's department store and apply for the Santa Claus position. I have all the qualifications: My name is Chris. I own a red velvet coat and pants. My cap has a white fringe and ball of white fur at the tip.

During my first year as a high school English teacher, I asked my class if they knew anyone who was a seamstress. Yes, one of the boys in the back row said. "My mother sews for extra money." The boy's mother drove to school, measured my arms and legs, and created a Santa Claus suit that deserves to be hung in the Smithsonian Institute right next to Mr. Rogers's sweater and Dorothy's ruby slippers.

Santa Claus is derived from the classical Dutch myth of Sinterklaas, whose name evolved from the Greek bishop Saint Nicholas. My parents were born in Belgium, on the Flemish side, and the Flemish people are really Dutch, so you see, I have Dutch blood streaming through my magical body. Of course I am Santa Claus!

Saint Nicholas, a fourth-century bishop, was known as a secret gift-giver, stuffing coins into the shoes of poor people who placed their shoes at their doorsteps. That tradition reconfigured itself into our Christmas stockings.

When I was a boy I wrapped pennies into a piece of cloth, tied the cloth at the four corners, and tossed my bag of *gold* into my sister's room when she wasn't looking or into my father's office while he was typing. I was a young Saint Nicholas, the rookie Santa Claus.

For many years, when my three children were little, I walked down the stairs each Christmas Eve in my Santa suit, bellowed "Ho-ho-ho," and watched the children run to me with open arms. Later, when "the children were nestled all snug in their beds, while visions of sugar plums danced in their heads," I stepped outside in the cold December night. There were stars usually, and sometimes snow, and I walked around the neighborhood. One time, a little boy was at his bedroom window. It was past midnight. The streetlight illuminated the boy's house. He looked down at me as I looked up at him through my beard and glasses, and he waved. I lifted my white gloved hand and waved back. The boy saw Santa Claus that night.

After my children grew up and moved out, I tucked my Santa suit away in the closet, and for years I just didn't think about my secret identity until my mother called one December afternoon to say that my father had had a stroke.

My father was never sick. He was ninety-five and healthy. I was not Clark Kent who could just zip into a phone booth and fly off to save my father, but "I am Santa Claus," I said to myself. I zoomed into the closet, grabbed my suit, and drove to my parents' house, the house where I grew up, the house where I was a boy, the house where my father built a wooden castle for me one Christmas, the house where my father pulled in the Christmas tree each year and anchored it in a bucket filled with stones.

After I pulled into the driveway, I slipped on my Santa suit in the car. Instead of walking to the front door and knocking, I thought it would have much more effect if I walked through the woods and appeared in the backyard ringing a bell, which is what I did.

As I stood in the woods alone, I looked at the snow that clung to the bushes and tree branches. I didn't feel like a fifty-five-year-old man but a boy who wanted to save his father. My fake beard itched; my black boots were not insulated. I just wanted to cry, thinking about my father's old body wearing down and about my children grown and gone and my powers as Kris Kringle waning, and then I saw the deer. Who would believe that I stood in the middle of the woods in my Santa Claus suit in the company of a deer? If it had a red nose I would have joined the skeptics and claimed that I was delirious.

After the deer ran off (probably afraid that I would try to harness it for my sleigh), I regained my powers, stepped out of the woods, and stood in the middle of the backyard, ringing the bell again and again with wide, swaying motions of my arm until my father came to the window in his wheelchair and waved. I stopped ringing my bell, stood in my red suit in the white snow, and waved back.

My father died anyway, although just a few years after that. The wave of Santa Claus's hand did not save him.

My Santa suit hangs in the closet like an old uniform that's seen better days of glory.

Now that I am on the way to my own old age in my wrinkled body, I hope people will say of me as Charles Dickens said of Scrooge: "It was always said of him, that he knew how to keep Christmas well, if any man alive possessed the knowledge."

I thought I had the knowledge. I guess I am not Santa Claus after all.

« »

When I doubt who I am,
when I doubt what I can give in love,
when I doubt how I can move forward,
I hear the Lord call my name,
and I am freshly baptized once again.

46

The Warmest Place on Earth

For unto us a child is born.
—Isaiah 9:6, KJV

Where is Christmas? Under the tree? In George Bailey's pocket next to Zuzu's petals?

In the 2000 movie *How the Grinch Stole Christmas* with this invective: "The avarice never ends! 'I want golf clubs. I want diamonds. I want a pony. . . .' Look, I don't wanna make waves, but this whole Christmas season is stupid."

We know where the word *Christmas* comes from. It is an Old English phrase, *Cristes moesse*, meaning the festival or mass of Christ. History tells us that in the middle of the fourth century there were all sorts of Christmas celebrations. Even before the development of the Christmas holiday, the time between December 25 and January 6 was considered holy in response to the changing seasons and to the fear of the long, dark nights.

When I was a boy, I wanted to hunt for Christmas with *Amahl and the Night Visitors* after they entered my house via the black-and-white television. In that little opera, the three kings were on their way looking for the Christ child. One of the kings asked the mother and the crippled boy, "Have you seen a Child, the color of wheat, the color of dawn? His eyes are mild, His hands are those of a King, as King He was born. Incense, myrrh, and gold we bring to His side, and the Eastern Star is our guide."

After seeing the story on television, I believed that the Eastern Star would be my guide and lead me to Christmas, so I grabbed my coat and boots and reached as far as the edge of the woods, and then I walked back into the house, discouraged and afraid of the dark.

I agree with the poet Dylan Thomas in the first line of his story *A Child's Christmas in Wales*, "One Christmas was so much like another." My children are grown. My father died in 2012. I am a bit tired of Christmas. All the activities connected to the holiday were once called traditions, but the older I get the more they seem like routines to play out once again. Where is Christmas? Maybe Christmas is hidden in the snowdrifts of Wales or in the Dutch shoes of Saint Nicholas.

Perhaps Christmas was found in the trenches of World War I in Belgium on December 25, 1914. My grandfather was a Belgian soldier in the war, and he told me many years ago when I was a boy that for reasons not fully understood, exhausted German troops began singing Christmas carols in their trenches, and then across No Man's Land, the exhausted British troops began also to sing Christmas carols in response to what they heard over the killing fields. Soon soldiers on both sides crawled out of their trenches and exchanged small gifts of alcohol, tobacco, food, and souvenirs of buttons from their uniforms.

But for me, the best road map to Christmas that I have seen this year is in the story of the baby boy that was abandoned in the crèche in a church in Queens, New York.

Can you imagine the sorrow and desperation this mother must have felt to give her baby up in such a way? First, she went to a dollar store to buy towels to keep the baby warm.

Can you imagine the harsh judgment the district attorney could have made against the mother? But instead he said that she had followed the spirit of New York's "Safe Haven" law. "It appears," the attorney said, "that the mother felt her newborn child would be safe in the church and chose to place the baby in the manger because it was the warmest place in the church."

A parish maintenance man discovered the child and quickly called for help, and the fire department rushed to the child's aid. The parish priest announced to his Sunday congregation that this baby carried a message of hope.

Perhaps this boy will grow up and be president someday, or a priest, or a firefighter, or a maintenance worker, or a compassionate district attorney, or a salesman in the dollar store.

Perhaps this boy will be a soldier or a poet. In his first week of life, he already accomplished a great thing: he led us all once again to the manger, the warmest place on earth.

« »

Blessed are the arms of the mother;
Blessed are the arms of the father.
Blessed are those who give comfort.

47

The Bear

The wolf will live with the lamb,
the leopard will lie down with the goat,
the calf and the lion and the yearling together,
and a little child will lead them.
The cow will feed with the bear,
their young will lie down together,
and the lion will eat straw like the ox.
—Isaiah 11:6–7

While I was driving on Route 287 on my way to my mother's house for dinner and a game of Scrabble, an SUV with a luggage rack attached to its rear zoomed past me to my left. Draped and bound over the rack was a large, dead black bear. Its fresh fur blew in waves under the wind of the traveling car. I saw one limp paw dangling from under the body of the large animal.

I understand the justification of culling the overpopulation of bears, but I suspect, too, that there are people who take pleasure in killing bears. I said to my mother as we opened the box of the Scrabble game, "I will never understand killing an animal for fun."

"People think differently from one another, Chris," my mother said as she picked out her seven letters.

Are we a fearful people? Do we take a gun and kill a bear to feel superior? To enjoy the hunt? To delight in the bragging rights?

This is the season to consider what is gentle. This is the season to consider what is hopeful and good in the face of what we fear.

When I was a boy, one of the local churches displayed a life-sized nativity. I remember being afraid of the large cow. Its head was bigger than half my body.

I didn't like the look of its horrible nose. When I looked at my mother, she suggested that I pick up a bit of loose straw and place it in the crib of the baby Jesus. I did. The cow didn't growl or stomp or swallow me whole.

Do you remember how Mister Rogers helped little children realize that they would not be sucked down into the drain? Do you remember Maurice Sendak's *Where the Wild Things Are* and how the ceiling of Max's bedroom turned into the world of vines and oceans? Do you remember the monsters with their terrible roars and gnashing teeth and their terrible eyes, and when Max yelled, "Be still!"

One of my favorite Christmas traditions as a boy was when my family and I watched the little opera *Amahl and the Night Visitors* by Gian Carlo Menotti. It is a story about the three kings on their way to see the Christ child, bearing gifts. The kings are tired and stay for a rest at the boy's house—the boy who is crippled, the boy who loves his mother.

I was a boy who loved his mother, but I was petrified of the three kings: their beards, their crowns, their gruff voices. But at one point the boy asks Balthazar, "Where's your home?" and the king kindly says, "I live in a black marble palace full of black panthers and white doves."

I liked that the king had panthers. I liked how panthers and doves could live together in a marble palace. Balthazar didn't seem so frightening after all.

My niece and nephew have a two-year-old son: Benjamin, who has red hair, the heart of an angel, and the energy of Superman. Benjamin was a bit intimidated with his visit to see Santa Claus, but when he touched Santa's gloved hand he was excited, less afraid, a boy suddenly filled with a sense for it all.

During this Christmas season, let's touch the hand of Santa Claus. Let's place a bit of straw at the foot of the manger. Let's build a place where panthers and doves roam together in peace. Let's tell the wild things in our lives to be still.

« »

Sing Noel, Noel. Sing peace, peace.
I pray in the season of light;
I pray in the season of the good news.

48

Silence

. . . a time to be silent . . .
—Ecclesiastes 3:7

As reported in *The New York Times* in 2012, "The rate of hearing loss among baby boomers is on average 31 percent lower than it was among our parents" in part because we have become more aware of workplace noises and we are in better health than the previous generation. But we are still succumbing to hearing loss, especially tinnitus, that annoying ringing in the ear that has no cure.

In Chaim Potok's beautiful novel *The Chosen*, a story of religion and the relationship between a father and son, a character says, "I've begun to realize that you can listen to silence and learn from it. It has a quality and a dimension all its own."

Do we value silence these days? The Transportation Department in New York City has decided to take down the "no honking" signs. Car companies are being encouraged to create fake noise in their electric cars—to protect pedestrians but also inadvertently serving to maintain the din we have created in our mechanized, chugging, noise-filled world.

The first time my brother-in-law spent several days at our small family cabin in Ontario, Canada, he couldn't sleep at night. "It was too quiet," John said with a chuckle.

If we choose to live, at times, a contemplative life, how do we mask the intruding sounds that surround us? Trappist monks, while not engaged in the popular notion of vows of silence, speak only when necessary as they try to refrain from idle talk. At meals they do not speak but, in their tradition, listen as a fellow monk reads aloud perhaps from a contemporary work of literature, perhaps from ancient poetry, or from a book of philosophy.

On June 6, 2002, beloved children's television host Fred Rogers gave the commencement address at Dartmouth College. There he told the young men and women, "I'd like to give you all an invisible gift. A gift of a silent minute to think about those who have helped you become who you are today." Hundreds of college graduates sat in silence with Mr. Rogers.

We yearn for silence when we are about to sleep. We enjoy the quiet time in our churches, mosques, temples, and synagogues.

Three years ago, I was sitting on the couch reading when I became annoyed with my neighbor. What was he doing? I heard a low ringing in the distance that was distracting me from my book. I stood up, walked outside to our small deck, and looked around. No power saws. No lawn mowers. No one was outside, and yet I kept hearing the subtle, annoying constant ringing.

I thought nothing of it until a few weeks later, when the ringing increased. Then I realized that the noise was not coming from the neighborhood but from inside my head.

After much cajoling from Roe, I visited an audiologist, and he said that I have what is called tinnitus and had lost enough of my hearing to warrant hearing aids. "The ringing in your ears," the doctor explained, "is a mechanism trying to compensate for that loss. The ringing will never go away, and might even increase."

What about silence? I wanted to ask the doctor. What about closing my eyes and hearing the voice of my grandmother? What about those hours in the middle of the night when I can't sleep and I want to imagine ice-skating as a child again with my sister as I try to hear the clicking of our skates on the smooth ice?

The doctor said that I could mask the ringing with a "white noise" machine that mimics wind or waterfalls. "This will mask the symptoms of tinnitus."

But I want the ability to lean back into *complete* silence. I do trick myself often as I imagine the ringing sounds a bit like crickets in August, which do soothe me to sleep easily. But crickets, waterfall, wind sounds—these are not silence, or stillness.

The doctor shrugged. "At least you are not Beethoven. He became completely deaf. Yes, he had complete silence, but think how horrible that must have been for the man who created the Ninth Symphony."

"Will I become deaf?"

"Perhaps," said the doctor. "Age advances."

We all have an inner voice—our mothers perhaps, God perhaps, Mr. Rogers even—and when we need to listen to these voices, we need a time of contemplation, a place of silence to sort things out.

In Potok's novel, the Rabbi tells his teenage son about silence: "It talks to me sometimes. I feel alive in it. It talks. And I can hear it."

While I will forever be denied complete silence, while the constant sound in my ears is the distant ringing knell of my own eventual death, I still feel alive in the companion of sound that does echo inside of my own heart as I listen to the imagined crickets in the middle of a North American winter.

« »

Remind me, Lord, today that if I listen carefully
I will hear the gentle whisper of your love and encouragement.

49

Communication

This is what the Lord, the God of Israel, says:
"Write in a book all the words I have spoken to you."
—Jeremiah 30:2

The Postal Service lost $5.1 billion in 2015, surrendering its core business to email and to online billing, and that makes me sad.

I remember running to the green mailbox at the end of the driveway when I was a boy, hoping there would be a birthday card from my grandmother. She always sent a card on my birthday, a five-dollar bill tucked inside.

In college, I opened my mailbox in the campus post office and reached into the little space without even looking, knowing that I would find letters from my fellow high school graduates and from my girlfriend.

I have lived for the past thirty-five years in Pompton Plains. John was our mailman for many of those years—John who always smiled, asked about the children, helped Roe with grocery bags, and kept tabs on who was sick in the neighborhood. Our current postman, Tommy, never misses waving a warm hello or, when it is raining, placing our mail behind the storm door instead of leaving it exposed to the weather.

Dylan Thomas in *A Child's Christmas in Wales* celebrated the postmen "with sprinkling eyes and wind-cherried noses."

Thomas understood that the mailmen "were just ordinary postmen, fond of walking and dogs and Christmas and the snow. They knocked on the doors with blue knuckles . . ." and Thomas remembered that the mailman wagged that wonderful, mysterious bag "like a frozen camel's hump."

There is no other profession whereby a human being comes to the door, smiles, knows my name, and hands me something another human being created.

I sent a card to my daughter in Portland, Oregon. The card left my hand and went into Tommy's hand. He sent it through the system, and the day before Valentine's Day, a human being handed my card to Karen. A letter hand delivered—hand to hand to hand—my hug across America to my daughter.

For the past sixty-four years of my life (except for Sundays) there's been mail practically every day: letters from my mother encouraging me to keep up my strength; pictures from my aunts in Belgium of their children and grandchildren; letters from former students, nieces, and nephews; letters from people all over the country who have read my books.

When a relative or a friend or an acquaintance picks up a pen and writes us a letter in his or her own penmanship, we have, for those moments, visual proof that this person devoted time and thoughts to us. I like holding a handwritten letter, a token from someone's desk and heart.

Today I receive email letters, e-birthday cards, and email Christmas letters. Receiving an email letter is like using binoculars to look at a painting. You see the real thing, but it is not a physical presence.

In a small box on my shelf are letters from Roe from when we first dated. John Updike sent me an encouraging letter, calling my essays "excellent and often very moving."

The Postal Service delivered to my doorstep a letter from President Ronald Reagan, who read in the White House about my severely disabled brother and wrote, "We sometimes fall into the habit of thinking that the weakest among us, like your brother Oliver, are a burden we must stoically bear. But you show that they can teach us the deepest lessons of love."

I treasure the letter of acceptance from Columbia University as I began my graduate work thirty-eight years ago, and I exchanged hundreds of letters with the children's television personality Mr. Rogers during our eighteen-year friendship.

Letters are consoling: "This is not a letter but my arms around you for a brief moment," Katherine Mansfield shared.

Letters allow us to live in the external world as we cherish our inner selves. Letters are humorous: Mark Twain is often quoted as having said, "I didn't attend the funeral, but I sent a nice letter saying I approved of it." Letters hold us together as a community: "Sir," John Donne insisted, "more than kisses, letters mingle souls."

I am sorry we are losing the charm and personal touch of actual letters. I can't place an email against my heart or have it on my chest when I wake up in the morning. I could print out an email, but to me it is a fake artifact.

It is far more wonderful finding the Rosetta Stone than it would be finding the code to the hieroglyphs printed out in an email from Egypt.

« »

By the words we shall know him
written on the fields in spring, on the sun in August,
against the harvest moon in autumn,
on the white pages of winter.
Blessed is the author of all things.

50

Gifts

Then they opened their treasures and presented him
with gifts of gold, frankincense and myrrh.
—Matthew 2:11

In Dylan Thomas's *A Child's Christmas in Wales*, he writes about useful Christmas presents: mittens, scarves, pictureless books, but then he also lists a few useless presents: candy jelly-babies, a false nose, a tram-conductor's cap, a celluloid duck, the snakes and ladders board game, and delicious caramels and marzipan.

As an adult I realize I ought to desire useful gifts for Christmas: a shirt and tie, a new electric razor, perhaps a new monitor for my computer, but I am also still a boy, and boys look forward to useless presents at Christmas. During the Christmases of my childhood, that treasure was hidden in my stocking and under the Christmas tree that sat in the middle of the living room like a forest jewel.

In August 1960, my grandmother from Belgium wrote to my mother, saying that she wanted to buy me a pair of shoes for Christmas—useful shoes—so my mother asked me to place my foot on a piece of paper, and then she traced my foot with a pencil. I wanted a cuckoo clock.

Sure enough, four months later, I opened my present from my grandmother: ugly black shoes that I or an undertaker wouldn't even wear. I would have been happy with a new pair of sneakers, Keds please, but no, my grandmother wanted to turn me into a little man, so there I sat beside the Christmas tree with serious-looking business wingtips with those little holes and deep shine. My younger brother got a little gray safe with a red combination dial!

But the next Christmas, when I was ten years old, I felt that enchantment of receiving a gift that was not only considered useless but also contained magic Christmas dust that still floats around me whenever I think of it.

In the late fall of that year, I was with my mother at the mall, and we strolled into a shop that sold, exclusively, merchandise from the Scandinavian countries: Norwegian sweaters, silver jewelry, clogs, and the brightly painted Swedish Dala horses carved from wood. And, on the shelf to the left of the door, a collection of Scandinavian wooden trolls. The one I liked most had a red cap, a painted apron on its chest, and a small, round nose. It was whimsical, suited my imagination concerning mythical beings, and it was $8.95. In 1961 dollars that was about $67.00.

When I voiced my delight about this small troll and told my mother how much I'd like that for Christmas, she looked at the price, lost her smile, and somewhere in the exchange of that silent moment, I knew that it was too expensive, and we left the store.

We have a long tradition of offering gifts. People in ancient Rome celebrated the harvest god's bounty at the end of the year with special foods and gift giving. In the fourth century, Nicholas the bishop became Saint Nicholas because he was known for his kindness and compassion for children. Whenever he could, he gave small gifts and sweets to the children of his town.

Fred Rogers of *Mister Rogers' Neighborhood* was my closest personal friend for eighteen years. We swam together off the Nantucket beach in Massachusetts, traveled together to Canada, exchanged letters and email messages nearly every day, and attended lectures at Lincoln Center in New York. He invited me to be on his children's television program; I sat on his porch swing as we talked about writing and children.

Fred often said to me that the best gift you can give someone is your complete honest self. During his hour-long Christmas television special in 1977 he said to his audience of children, "I've been thinking about what I'd like to give you for Christmas. I'd really like to give you something that just fits your own wishes and needs the way these shoes just fit me. I suppose the thing I'd like most to be able to give you is hope. Hope that through your own doing and your own living with others, you'll be able to find what best fits for you in this life."

For my fiftieth birthday, Fred gave me a set of gold cuff links. "These were my father's," he said, "and he gave these to me for my birthday, and now I want to pass them along to you."

Fred Rogers died from stomach cancer on February 27, 2003. On January 3, 2003, I received my last email from Fred, in which he wrote, in part, "Thank you again and again and again for the gift of all your prayers. That's the kind of sustenance I'm needing every minute of every day and night."

On December 25, 1961, a ten-year-old boy sat next to his mother as she helped him open a white cardboard box. The boy reached inside the box, carefully felt through the crinkly tissue paper, and pulled out a Swedish troll with a red cap, a painted apron on its chest, and a small, round nose.

I am giving those gold cuff links to my son this Christmas.

A small fifty-two-year-old wooden troll sits on my shelf here in this small room where I write.

We try our best, on December 25, to create a beautiful day in our neighborhoods for our children. No matter what religion we consider, we can all subscribe to peace on earth, goodwill toward all people.

Fred Rogers taught me that, in the end, the most useful gifts are the ones tied with the bows of love.

« »

For those who lack gifts, we pray for you.
For those who are generous, we thank you.

51

Memories of the Crèche

So they hurried off and found Mary and Joseph, and the baby,
who was lying in the manger.
—Luke 2:16

When I first heard the word *crèche* as a boy, I thought it was the name of some sort of new soda. I didn't know it meant the Christmas manger or, as I learned in Catholic school, the Nativity. But I was not confused about the role the crèche played in my Christmas days of long ago.

Each December, my father pulled up from the basement a large metal tray. I learned years later that this was just an old oven tray that he had kept after my parents replaced the kitchen oven, but to me, this oven tray was the bedrock of Bethlehem.

"Who would like to help me build the Nativity?" my father asked each winter. My sisters, brothers, and I knew what was needed: moss, small rocks, twigs, and sand. We'd run outside in our hand-me-down winter coats, in our mismatched gloves, and scour the yard and woods for just the right stones and just the right moss, and then we'd rush to the kitchen, where our father stood beside the kitchen table. On it he had placed the large tray.

I liked so much watching as my father spread sand on the tray, and then he'd place the rocks we had collected to make a small cave, and the moss was the hills and the sticks were trees. Then my mother would step into the kitchen with a metal Christmas box filled with shepherds, sheep, Mary, Joseph, the baby Jesus, and a small crib, and Bethlehem once again appeared in our house for the holiday season.

The word *crèche*, an old French word, ultimately derived from the German word for "crib," and so from tradition to tradition and language to language we have inherited the modern image of the manger. Roe and I wanted to create our own traditions, so we decided to create our own version of the crèche, using our children.

Michael was nine months old (a perfect baby Jesus), Karen (a spitting image of Mary) was three, and David (a perfect Joseph) was five years old.

We hung a brown blanket over the windows of the small sun porch attached to our house. Karen's veil was a blue towel; her dress was one of my T-shirts. David wore my belt as a headband and a brown towel over another of my T-shirts. He liked the large stick we found that he used as his staff. And Michael, we just wrapped him in a receiving blanket. We borrowed from the church a small crib that was used on Christmas Eve. We bought a bale of hay from a garden center, cut out a yellow star to hang above the scene, and there we were, standing before the crèche in Pompton Plains, New Jersey, in 1985.

I don't care too much for the life-sized plastic crèches we see illuminated on people's lawns. I confess that I wasn't always crazy about the live manger scenes either. When I was a boy, my father and I visited a live crèche at the Methodist church that frightened me when Joseph turned, looked directly at me, and said hello.

In 1985, the United States Supreme Court allowed the crèche to be displayed on public property because there was "insufficient evidence to establish that the inclusion of the crèche is a purposeful or surreptitious effort to express some kind of subtle governmental advocacy of a particular religious message."

The crèche, in the end, is all about a boy who grew up over two thousand years ago, who then went on to make a huge impact on how we human beings treat one another.

May you build your own nativity scenes with moss and stones. May all your future days blend joyously as we reach back each night to Bethlehem.

« »

Blessed is the Christ child with us all.
Blessed is the Holy Family with us all.
Blessed is the Light of the World, for he is in us.

52

Sitting with the Nostalgia of Winter

And I will still be carrying you when you are old.
Your hair will turn gray, and I will still carry you.
I made you, and I will carry you to safety.
—Isaiah 46:4, ERV

It is one thing to sit in my warm winter house with a book on my lap, staring at the ice cubes bobbing in a glass of water in my old, wrinkled hand, and another thing to feel the pull of memories about being a boy who delighted in his relationship with winter and ice.

Part of being a boy in winter was being cold with red cheeks, wearing wide black boots, and pretending to be a dragon as the mist from my mouth came out looking like smoke. I made my way to invade the kingdom of the garage and steal icicles.

In one postcard winter of long ago I discovered that the garage was where the best icicles hung because there were no gutters. I grabbed a stick (my lance, of course) and tapped an icicle until it wiggled free like a loose tooth and fell into my hands.

I took my icicle and ran into the house to create my own winter treat. I opened the lid of the sugar container, poked the tip of the icicle into the sugar, and licked my ice-candy stick with delight and pride, thinking how clever I was to create such a delicious concoction. But a boy is a king until his mother approaches the kitchen and the boy runs out the back door and retreats to Wonderland, or to Narnia.

The swamp behind the woods was my Wonderland, my escape from the ordinary world of brothers and sisters, cats and television. This was the place, especially in winter, where snow was whiter and ice thicker, where small children ice-skated past bulrushes and the big kids played hockey.

Each time I visited the swamp in winter I knelt and began rubbing my glove onto the ice, polishing it as if it was a magic lantern. The ice was magic when it was translucent, and I saw goldfish swimming under me like dancing Japanese women with their orange flowing robes and orange fans.

In winter, it seems, kids like to make their mark, leaving behind evidence that they were there. We fell backward and created angels in the white drifts of snow. We threw snowballs against the side of the house, leaving a temporary white stain honoring our marksmanship. I liked taking my hand and pressing it against the ice on the living room window, leaving my handprint on the glass.

Today I attack the ice on my brick steps with blends of sodium chloride, calcium chloride, or magnesium chloride—all salt, the enemy of ice. I vigorously chop it with a thick blade at the end of a long handle and, with force, rake it off the windshield of my car with a hard-plastic scraper. I do violence on the ice that covers my driveway, but then in my quiet time, I am back on the couch, and the book on my lap comes alive.

Alice, in Lewis Carroll's *Through the Looking-Glass*, is talking to her cat and says, "Do you hear the snow against the window-panes, Kitty? How nice and soft it sounds! Just as if someone was kissing the window all over outside. I wonder if the snow *loves* the trees and fields, that it kisses them so gently?"

The memories of winter and ice kiss me gently as I pick up my book and pause for a moment longer and think that perhaps smooth ice is a path to paradise, and then I adjust my glasses, open my book, and continue reading.

« »

Covet love. Covet a warm blanket and a book on your lap.
There is more to our silence and old age than in the beating
of our hearts,
So let us dream, pray, rest, and prepare our way to the Lord
with confidence.

53

Angels

Behold, I send an Angel before thee,
to keep thee in the way, and to bring thee
into the place which I have prepared.
—Exodus 23:20, KJV

My brother Oliver died in my mother's arms, of pneumonia. After bathing him in bed with a sponge for thirty-two years, after feeding him with a spoon for thirty-two years, after pulling down the shade each morning so the rising sun did not burn his tender skin, our mother watched Oliver take his last breath. She whispered, "Goodbye, my angel."

When I was a boy, it was my job to feed Oliver dinner: a raw egg, baby cereal, sugar, and a banana pureed inside a red ceramic bowl my father had received one Christmas filled with plum pudding. I never needed a watch because I always had an instinctual feeling that it was time to feed Oliver, and I never missed. If I was playing baseball on the front lawn in the summer, or sledding down the neighbor's hill in the winter, I'd suddenly call out "Gotta go! Gotta feed Oliver!" and I'd abandon my position at third base or grab my sled and rush home.

Oliver was blind. Once I thought that maybe he was faking it, so I sneaked up on him and waved my hand right in his face. He never blinked.

Oliver couldn't talk, read, or sing. The doctors, after many tests, convinced my parents that Oliver had no intellect, no possible way of learning anything due to severe brain damage before he was born.

My brother was on his back in his bed for thirty-two years. His bed was against the yellow wall, and my father built a low barrier made of plywood on the other side so Oliver would not roll out. Oliver never moved by himself. He was rolled back and forth and bathed each day. He never had a bedsore.

We never know how sorrows of the past will influence us in the future. When Oliver was born, my parents were devastated. With each passing day they learned more and more of Oliver's afflictions: unable to lift his head, unable to chew or walk or grow up to be the president of the United States. So instead they just chose to call Oliver their son and they chose to love him.

Because of that single decision, I was given a guardian angel, and I didn't realize it until many years later.

I liked watching how gently my father shaved Oliver and combed his hair. I liked helping my sister carry Oliver to the bathtub. I liked propping Oliver up with my hand behind his head as I gently touched the rim of the glass to his lips and watched as he slowly drank the cold milk.

Oliver learned to do two things: raise his crooked arms up and down and laugh. That is all. Sometimes in the middle of the night I could hear his belly laughter echoing down the hall. My grandmother often said that Oliver was laughing with the angels.

Often when I am tired after a long day, I rub my face and think of Oliver's deep, brown eyes. When I pour a bowl of cereal in the morning before trudging off to work, I often think of Oliver's red bowl that I carried up to his room all those years as a boy.

Remember that charming film *As Good as It Gets*, where Melvin, played by Jack Nicholson, says to Carol the waitress, played by Helen Hunt: "You make me want to be a better man"?

Oliver made me a better man. I have been a father, teacher, and writer. Through my brother's helplessness he taught me how to help children in need. Through his silence he pointed out how to be a poet. Through Oliver's hunger he showed me, like Merlin, how to mix life in a red bowl. Oliver was my guardian angel.

The Islamic tradition speaks about the *raqib*: the watcher, their angel who protects them throughout their lives. The Buddhist lamas teach that the devas are angel-like, ethereal beings who applaud our goodness, rejoice when we are well, and rain flowers over us when we struggle.

In Judaism the angel Lailah protects pregnant woman at night and serves as guardian angels to everyone and guides their souls to heaven.

Christians believe, as Pope Francis said in 2014, "No one journeys alone and no one should think that they are alone." And he acknowledged that the voice of our guardian angel is always within us, whispering wisdom and comfort during our times of distress.

I wish the world could rub the sponge onto Oliver's tender skin and feed him from the depth of the red bowl and give him milk. I wish we could all stand at his bedroom door together as a civilization at midnight during these times of distress and hear Oliver laugh.

On my brother's tombstone my mother wrote, "Blessed are the pure of heart, for they shall see God." May your guardian angel help you see God, Allah, Buddha, Abraham, Christ. May we all sleep in peace and laugh at midnight.

George Eliot wrote, in her novel *Silas Marner*, "In old days there were angels who came and took men by the hand and led them away from the city of destruction. We see no white-winged angels now."

Perhaps Oliver could guide us all out of the cities of destruction. I wish I could carry Oliver to Bethlehem, to Mecca, to the Wailing Wall, to the Buddha, to the temple, mosque, and church and have the world touch Oliver's hand.

« »

I pray that those who are weak continue to teach those who are strong.

54

On Valentine's Day

I am my beloved's and my beloved is mine.
—Song of Solomon 6:3

Konrad Lorenz was the famous Austrian naturalist who won a Nobel Prize in science, in part because of his observations of geese. He learned that when a brood of goslings hatch, they socially bond to the first nurturing thing they encounter. Typically, of course, they bond with the mother goose, but Lorenz discovered that they would also bond with him.

They followed him everywhere. When he walked, the entire brood scurried along behind him like kindergartners. When he paddled in his kayak, the small birds swam alongside. When he ran, the birds ran with him.

Lorenz studied this phenomenon much of his life, which helped him develop the theory he called imprinting, the attachment a newborn animal makes with its caregiver: a mother goose, a hen, or in Lorenz's case, a man. In human beings, I call this imprinting infatuation.

Remember the famous cartoon skunk Pepé Le Pew, created by Chuck Jones? Upon seeing Penelope for the first time, Pepé Le Pew is immediately besotted. Of course, the infatuated skunk doesn't realize that Penelope is a black cat with an accidental white stripe down her back because she just squeezed under a freshly painted white fence.

Many people "fall in love" with an image or with an idea and not with the reality of the other person. Look at silly Romeo in William Shakespeare's play. In the first act, his friend Benvolio is worried. It seems Romeo is ill, lovesick over a beautiful girl. He tells his friend this girl is exquisite, beautiful, fair, and when she dies, all of beauty will dim with her.

Romeo laments that this girl is not interested in him, and he cries that "she'll not be hit with Cupid's arrow."

Everyone who reads the play for the first time thinks, of course, that Romeo is speaking about Juliet. But no, Romeo is pining for Rosaline, someone Romeo simply imprinted on for her beauty, while not knowing anything else about her. Benvolio tries to help Romeo snap out of his grief and suggests that Romeo "examine other beauties."

Of course, at the evening masquerade ball, Romeo sees someone new, and he falls madly in love simply upon seeing Juliet for the first time. He asks a servant, "What lady is that, which doth enrich the hand of yonder knight?"

The puzzled servant doesn't have a clue, but it is too late. Romeo imprints himself on the image of Juliet.

> O, she doth teach the torches to burn bright!
> It seems she hangs upon the cheek of night
> Like a rich jewel in an Ethiope's ear;
> Beauty too rich for use, for earth too dear!
> So shows a snowy dove trooping with crows,
> As yonder lady o'er her fellows shows.
> The measure done, I'll watch her place of stand,
> And, touching hers, make blessed my rude hand.
> Did my heart love till now? forswear it, sight!
> For I ne'er saw true beauty till this night.

Wait a minute. Just this morning, Romeo was madly in love with Rosaline, and now, within minutes, he sees this young woman Juliet and he is in love with her!

Men and women are easily swayed by the illusion of love. "Ah, but I love Penelope," Pepé Le Pew says. "Come to me, my beauty. I romance you with my kisses. But what is this? You are a cat! What is this white paint on your back!"

While plenty of relationships end when the paint is discovered or fades, for some people, false love never fades for it is a powerful illusion that doesn't let go.

Look at poor Gatsby in F. Scott Fitzgerald's novel *The Great Gatsby*. Gatsby met Daisy when they were both young. Gatsby loved the Daisy he created in his mind. When they separated, he built up in his mind more and more the vision of this woman. He became rich simply to attract Daisy, to win her back when, in the end, the Daisy he had built in his mind never existed.

During their reunion, Gatsby couldn't see that Daisy was a superficial, spoiled, selfish woman. He could not escape the "vitality of his illusion," as Fitzgerald wrote. For years, ever since he latched on to the dream of Daisy, he threw himself upon that dream with "creative passion." And then Fitzgerald says with sadness, "No amount of fire or freshness can challenge what a man will store in his ghostly heart."

Valentine's Day is a time to reflect on our own definition of love and to define what is stored in our souls.

Candy hearts and a dozen roses fill in the superficial social expectations of affection on such a day, but what is love? Tevye in *Fiddler on the Roof* asks his wife, Golde, "Do you love me?"

Golde answers, "You're a fool!"

Tevye answers that he agrees, and many husbands do feel that they're fools, but still, he wants to hear the answer. So Golde goes into her famous rant that for twenty-five years she has cleaned, cooked, tended to the children, and milked the cow. Isn't that proof enough?

But the man persists: "I know. But do you love me?" And of course, Golde eventually relents and says, tenderly, "I suppose I do." And together in song, Tevye and Golde admit that it is "nice to know."

Infatuation, imprinting, love at first sight, Hallmark cards, boxes of candy. Valentine's Day is no different from any other day, but it is a good day to tell someone you love them not because of a dream, beauty, or illusions, but just because you do. We all can agree that it is nice to know.

《 》
I pray for those I love.
I pray for those who cannot love.
Blessed are we who hear the good news.
Thank you, Jesus, for your message:
"Love one another."

55

Love

Love bears all things, believes all things,
hopes all things, endures all things.
—1 Corinthians 13:7, ESV

It is believed that Geoffrey Chaucer, the fourteenth-century poet, created the tradition of Valentine's Day more than seven centuries ago with his poem "In the Parliament of Fowls," a poem about love in the king's court. It reads in part "You know that on Saint Valentine's day, / By my statute and through my governance, /You come to choose—and then fly your way—/ Your mates."

February is a good time of year to remember how we chose our mates and flew off into our destinies together.

My mother, who is ninety-five, just celebrated the seventy-second anniversary of her wedding to my father, who died in 2012 at the age of 100. How she met my father is part of my family's lore and something I always think about on February 14.

At the end of World War II, my mother wanted to go to Paris with her father, and he emphatically said, "No! I will be on a military train." My grandfather was a general in the Belgian army and part of the delegation sent to France by his superiors to help reorganize war-torn Europe.

My mother, twenty-three at the time, had spent four years under Nazi occupation, so she relished the opportunity to travel to Paris.

"No. Impossible," my grandfather insisted, but then my grandmother had an idea. She took one of my grandfather's old uniforms and stitched here and there until it fit my mother.

My grandfather looked at my mother as she stood in her green corporal's uniform and tipped hat, and then he smiled. So my mother accompanied my grandfather as his military aide. Of course there were no female military aides to Belgian officers in 1945, but no one stopped my grandfather as he and my mother stepped into the train to Paris. No one stopped them as they ate at the American military canteen, where my mother had white bread for the first time in four years.

In Paris, my mother and grandfather stayed in a hotel without heat, this being the winter of 1945, and my mother remembers being so cold at night that she wrapped herself in the hotel rug in an effort to keep warm under her blanket.

What does a twenty-three-year-old Belgian girl do in Paris while her father is attending government meetings all day long? "I walked and walked just to stay warm. I visited the museums and the cathedrals, but everything was gloomy and cold. I was miserable," my mother said.

My grandfather, recognizing that it had been a mistake to bring his daughter, asked a business associate if he knew someone who could entertain my mother. "Yes, I will send my assistant."

The "assistant" was a thirty-three-year-old man who lived like the Great Gatsby, waltzed every weekend, enjoyed pheasant hunting, and wanted nothing to do with entertaining the child of a Belgian officer. But the boss insisted, so this disgruntled man who practically lived in a tuxedo the first thirty years of his life trudged to the hotel in the cold winter air.

When he met my mother, he did not tell her that he was a Belgian baron. He did not tell her about the size of his summer and winter estates. He didn't speak about the chauffeurs, the gardeners, the washerwomen, the cooks, and the private tutors; all he did was invite my mother to walk along the River Seine that to this day still flows in and out of my imagination.

The general's daughter and the baron discovered, immediately, the *bouquinistes*, the used book stalls that have been there for more than four hundred years. Many people still refer to the Seine as the only river in the world that runs between two bookshelves.

They also quickly discovered that they had the same interests in books and authors.

"Look at this book of poems," the young man said. "No one knows about his work. He is so obscure. This is a book I must have," and so he bought it.

"I love his poetry," my mother said.

As they walked to the next book stall, my mother found a novel she had always wanted to read, and she bought it. The young man practically knew the book by heart.

At the third book stall, my mother and her companion reached for the same book about the fourteenth-century Italian writer and mystic Angela of Foligno. They both wanted to buy this book, and the man said, "Well, if we both want it, the only thing to do is to buy it together and get married."

In three days my parents were engaged, and three months later they were married.

On October 9, 2013, Pope Francis declared Angela a saint, and it was Saint Angela who wrote so many hundreds of years ago: "Because of love, and in it, the soul first grows tender."

I will never forget how tenderly my mother tipped the small shovel of dirt over my father's open grave.

« »

Let me remember those who have loved one another.
Let me tell the stories of love; let me explain
the power of tenderness in the name of the Lord,
in the name of the compassionate God in heaven.

56

I'm Growing Old, I Delight in the Past

Even to your old age and gray hairs I am he, I am he who will sustain you. I have made you and I will carry you; I will sustain you and I will rescue you.
—Isaiah 46:4

The new year is my sixty-seventh, and with age I have come to understand that no matter how hard I try to hold on to the past, the images fade and will, eventually, disappear.

When I was a boy, my Belgian grandmother visited our home in Allendale, New Jersey, nearly every summer. She brought Belgian chocolates, her felt hat, and thick-heeled shoes. We played cards, sang French songs, and sat in the yard together. She came to my college graduation and later pushed my son in a carriage.

In the fall of 1981, my parents and I helped my grandmother into a wheelchair and kissed her goodbye at Newark airport. The thoughtful airline worker who took hold of the chair kindly turned it around and pulled my grandmother backward toward two wide doors. The doors opened automatically. My grandmother sat in the wheelchair with her felt hat, and she waved goodbye. I never saw her again. Her worn heart gave out, and she died that winter.

When my daughter Karen married a number of years ago, she and her husband decided that they wanted to move to Portland, Oregon, and they were going to rent a U-Haul truck and drive across the country. As the day of their departure approached, I was excited for them: a grand trip across the United States! And when they pulled out of the driveway, I ran to the street and waved and waved, watching the orange and white truck grow smaller and smaller. Just before the truck turned and disappeared, Karen stuck her hand out the window and waved goodbye.

That night I was so happy for her. Two days later I said to myself, "Karen was here just two days ago." As the weeks progressed, I said to my wife, "Karen was here just a month ago." It took time for me to realize that things would never be as they once were. Karen is living outside Portland with her husband. She is happy. She has found her way. I held her hand when she stepped into the ocean for the first time, when her mother took a photograph of us before her senior prom, and when I led her down the aisle on her wedding day. I will never forget her hand waving out the window of that U-Haul truck, a truck that just seemed, on its own, to turn and disappear.

One afternoon when I was a teenager, I was thumbing through a family album, and I came across a small photo of a dock at some old seaport town. My father walked into the living room, and he said, "Look closely. What do you see on the dock?"

I squinted a bit and said that I saw a man waving. "That is my father. He came to the pier in Belgium with your mother and me as we were leaving for America in 1948." They were on the boat, waving goodbye.

I looked up at my father. He looked at me and said, "That was the last time I saw him."

When my son was eight, he asked me if I knew anyone who was old and lived in Australia. I said no, and asked why he wanted to know. "Well, if we did, when that person dies he can tell us if there is a heaven."

If you are an eight-year-old boy, you might think that Australia is already halfway to heaven, and you might want an explanation about what happens to us—all of us—when we disappear.

I agree with the artist Henri Matisse, who once said, later in life, "I'm growing old, I delight in the past."

My past is connected to wheelchairs, rented trucks, and photographs in the family album, but the older I get, the harder they are to see. Perhaps I am already on my own journey to Australia.

« »

Though I see the light of my life dimming, Lord,
though I see the approaching shadows,
grant me continued vision of your embrace
as I enter your kingdom of heaven.

Acknowledgments

I would like to acknowledge, with gratitude, the following people who have greatly contributed to the editing of this book during the five years of my writing these essays: Melene Kubat, Peter Grad, Marcia Lythcott, and Bruce Lowry.

I would also like to acknowledge, with gratitude, both Joe Durepos, the acquisition editor at Loyola Press who took on this work with immediate enthusiasm; and to Joellyn Cicciarelli, President of Loyola Press, who also felt an immediate response to the hope expressed in this small volume.

Much gratitude is also extended to Maria Cuadrado, Director of Trade Books, and Rob Ferry, Project Manager for their guidance and professionalism, and to Vinita Wright for her stunning skills as an editor who shared my vision for this work.

On September 16, 1992, at the Marguerite Bourgeoys Family Service Foundation in Montreal, Henri Nouwen said, "Gratitude flows from the recognition that who we are and what we have are gifts to be received and shared." I am deeply grateful to Loyola Press for the opportunity to reaffirm in this book that who we are and what we have are all gifts that stem from compassion, forgiveness, joy, and love—these gifts bestowed upon us from a merciful God.

About the Author

After graduating from Columbia University with a doctorate in education, **Christopher de Vinck** married Rosemary. They have been together 43 years and counting and have raised three children. A 40-year veteran of high school teaching and administration, de Vinck has written twelve books, publishing with Viking, Doubleday, HarperCollins, Crossroad Books, Paulist Press, and Loyola Press.

De Vinck's essays have been widely published in *The New York Times*, *The Chicago Tribune*, *The Wall Street Journal*, *USA Today*, and *The National Catholic Reporter*. He is a national spokesman for the disabled and the power of the powerless, having given talks based on his Doubleday book and his essay in *The Wall Street Journal* about how his disabled brother influenced the president of the United States, the pope in Rome, and millions of people who met Oliver through Christopher's books, essays, and speaking engagements.